SAN FRANCISCO

W9-CEJ-515

KNOPF MAPGUIDES

Welcome to San Francisco!

This opening fold-out contains a general map of San Francisco to help you visualize the 6 large districts discussed in this guide, and 4 pages of valuable information, handy tips and useful addresses.

Discover San Francisco through 6 districts and 6 maps

A Marina / Fisherman's Wharf / Russian Hill

B North Beach / Financial District / Chinatown

C Embarcadero / Union Square / South of Market

D Nob Hill / Pacific Heights / Civic Center

E Haight Ashbury / Castro / The Mission

F The Presidio / Richmond / Lincoln Park

For each district there is a double-page of addresses (restaurants – listed in ascending order of price – cafés, bars, music venues and stores) followed by a fold-out map for the relevant area with the essential places to see (indicated on the map by a star ★). These places are by no means all that San Francisco has to offer but to us they are unmissable. The grid-referencing system (**A** B2) makes it easy for you to pinpoint addresses quickly on the map.

Transport and hotels in San Francisco

The last fold-out consists of a transport map and 4 pages of practical information that include a selection of hotels.

Thematic index

Lists all the sites and addresses featured in this guide.

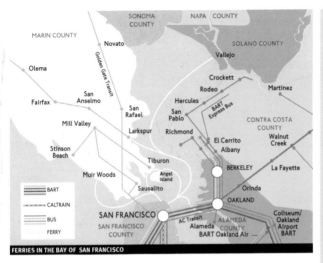

FERRIES IN THE BAY OF SAN FRANCISCO

MUSEUMS

Opening hours
Usually open from 10am to 5pm. Closed on Mon.
City Pass Card
→ *Museum ticket offices, Visitor Information Center. Price $36 (9 days)*
Unrestricted access to six museums or attractions (Exploratorium, California Palace of Legion of Honor, SF MoMA, California Academy of Sciences, Blue and Gold Bay Cruise, Steinhart Aquarium).
Free entry
Free 1st Wed of the month: Exploratorium, Asian Art Museum, African American Museum. The rest are free the 1st Thu of the month.

SHOPPING

Opening hours
Stores open Mon-Sat 10am-6pm; Sun noon-5pm.
In Chinatown, daily 10am-10pm. Department stores open Mon-Sat 10am-8pm; Sun noon-6pm.
Department stores
Macy's (**C** B2)
→ *170 O'Farrell St/Stockton St*
Tel. 397 3333
Saks Fifth Avenue (**C** B2)
→ *384 Post / Powell sts*
Tel. 986 4300
San Francisco
Shopping Center (**C** B3)
→ *865 Market St /5th St*
Tel. 495 5656
Sales
Twice a year, the first two weeks of January and at the end of June.
Taxes
There is an 8.25% tax on the marked price for most standard consumer goods (clothes, hi-fi, video...)

MARKETS

Flea Market at 1651
Mission (**D** C5)
→ *Van Ness Ave / Mission St*
Sat-Sun 6am-4.30pm
Second-hand clothes, hi-fi bargains and hidden treasures.
Sutter St Flea Market (**C** B2)
→ *567 Sutter St*
An antiques market, one block from Union Square.
Flower Mart (**C** C4)
→ *6th St (between Brannan and Bryant sts)*
Mon-Sat 10am-3pm
Huge flower market in the heart of SoMa (South of Market).
Heart of the City (**D** C-D4)
→ *Market St between 7th and 8th sts*
Tel. 558 9455
Sun 7am-5pm;
Wed 7am-5.30pm
Fresh fruit and vegetables, olives, dried fruit.
Ferry Plaza Farmer's
Market (**C** D1)
→ *Embarcadero/Market St*
Tue 10am-2pm
→ *Embarcadero/Green*
Sat-Sun 8am-2pm
Flowers and fresh vegetables from local farmers.

SAN FRANCISCO AND ITS WRITERS

Via Ferlinghetti, Jack Kerouac Alley, City Lights Bookstore... And relics of the Beat Generation in the North Beach neighborhood.
Vesuvio Café (B B4)
→ *255 Columbus Ave ((between Broadway and Pacific Avenue)*
Tel. 362 3370
Daily 6am-2am
Once the HQ of the Beat Generation, this two-floor bar has the atmosphere of a Parisian bistro (small wooden tables, old photos of writers on the walls, jazz in the back-ground). For all Kerouac fans. Coffee $1.

EXOTIC SAN FRANCISCO

Chinatown (B B5-6)
Dim sum, mahjong, Buddhist temples, Tai Chi, exotic fruit stalls, herbalists and pagoda-style roofs in the second largest Chinese neighborhood outside Asia.
North Beach (B A4)
Italian enclave around Washington Square, dotted with trattorias, cafés and delicatessens.
The Mission District (E F3)
Tacos and murals in the pulsing heart of Hispanic San Francisco.
Japantown (D A-B3)
Sushi bars, teahouses, Buddhist and Shinto temples, Japanese architecture, including a genuine pagoda.

Welcome to San Francisco!

GOLDEN GATE NATIONAL RECREATION AREA

GOLDEN GATE BRIDGE

FORT POINT

PACIFIC OCEAN

GOLDEN GATE NATIONAL RECREATION AREA

PARADE GROUND

SAN FRANCISCO NATIONAL MILITARY CEMETERY

PRESIDIO GOLF COURSE

MOUNTAIN LAKE PARK

F

LINCOLN PARK

CLIFF HOUSE

POINT LOBOS AV.

GEARY

F

CALIFORNIA STREET

PARK PRESIDIO BLVD.

GEARY STREET

BOULEVARD

BALBOA

STREET

RICHMOND

FULTON STREET

CALIFORNIA ACADEMY OF SCIENCE

GOLDEN GATE PARK

GREAT HIGHWAY

LINCOLN WAY

LINCOLN WAY

JUDAH SUNSET STREET

19TH

7TH AVENUE

SUNSET

NORIEGA STREET

AVENUE

E

PARKSIDE

BOULEVARD

TARAVAL STREET

GREAT HIGHWAY

PINE LAKE PARK

SLOAT BOULEVARD

ST. FRANCIS WOODS

PORTOLA DR.

DEWEY BLVD.

OCEAN AVENUE

GOLDEN GATE NATIONAL RECREATION AREA

SKYLINE BLVD.

19TH AV.

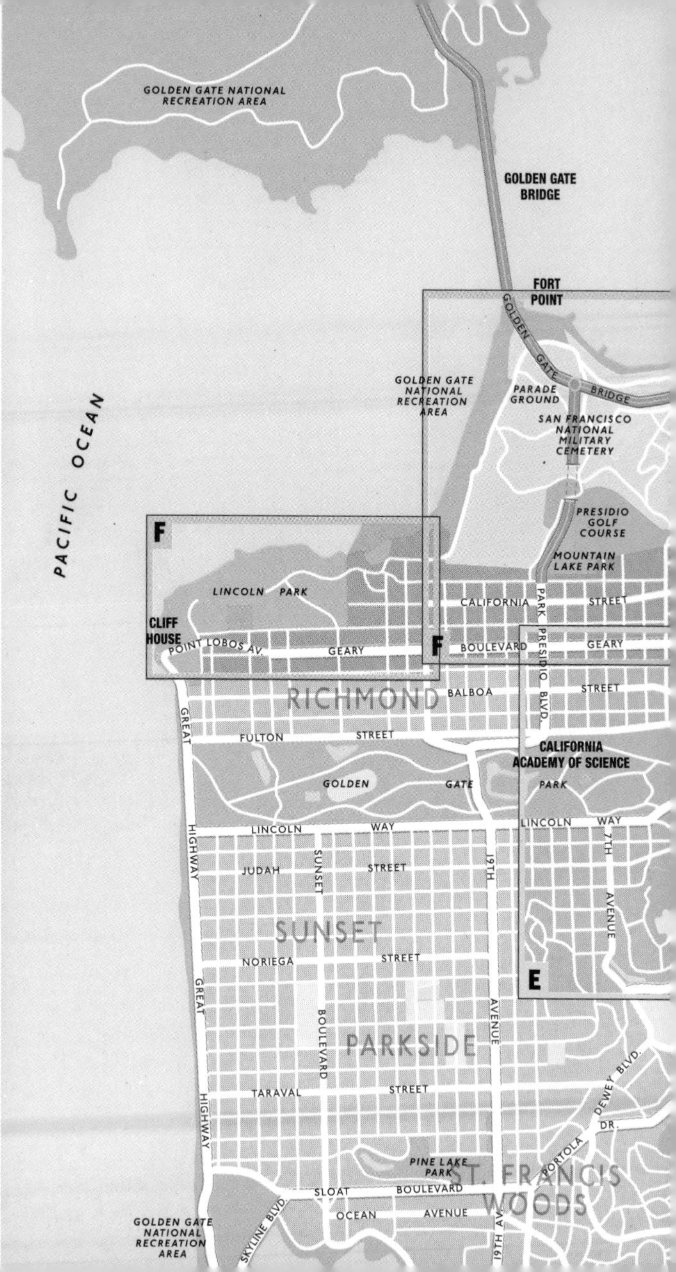

CITY PROFILE

- 757,000 inhabitants
- Surface area of 45 sq. miles ■ 16 million visitors per year ■ 43 hills ■ 4th largest city in California, after Los Angeles, San Diego and San Jose.

CLIMATE

- Spring/summer: 49–65 °F (9–18 °C), frequent fog ■ Autumn: 54–68 °F (12–20 °C), clear sky ■ Winter: 47–62 °F (8–17 °C), rain.

TIME DIFFERENCE

Noon in London = 4am in San Francisco

VIEW FROM THE TOP OF TELEGRAPH HILL

VIEWS OF THE CITY

Alamo Square (E E1)
The most beautiful cluster of Victorian houses, against the backdrop of skyscrapers.
Twin Peaks (E D4)
Unique 360° panoramic view of San Francisco from the top of these two unspoiled hills.
Telegraph Hill (B B3)
Spectacular view of North Beach, the bay and the city's many hills.
Golden Gate Bridge (F B1)
The famous steel giant, 220 ft above the Golden Gate channel and the rocky shore.

SPORTS & LEISURE

Golden Gate Park (E C2)
Tennis
→ Tel. 753 7001 (bookings) John F. Kennedy and Middle drives.
Boating
→ Stow Lake / Tel. 752 0347 Rental of rowboats, pedal boats and motor boats.
Golf
→ Golf Course, 47th Ave / John F. Kennedy Drive Tel. 751 8987 Beautiful 9-hole course.
Horse riding
→ 36th Ave / John F. Kennedy Dr. Tel. 668 7360 Starting point at the Golden Gate Park Stables.
Beaches
Baker Beach (F A3)
→ Gibson Road, off Lincoln Blvd The Presidio beach front: dunes, wind and surf.
China Beach (F B4)
→ At the end of Sea Cliff Ave Swimming protected from

the winds of the bay.
Ocean Beach
→ Great Highway (between Balboa St and Sloat Blvd) Promenade bordering a long sandy beach on the Pacific Coast.

ALTERNATIVE SAN FRANCISCO

By hydroplane
SF Seaplane Tours
→ Departs from Pier 39 Tel. 332 4843 / Price $129 (30 mins); $159 (40 mins) Spectacular flight over the Bay Area and the city's prettiest neighborhoods.
By boat
Red and White Fleet Bay Cruise
→ Pier 43 Tel. 1 877 855 5506 Daily 10am–6.15pm; $20 Tour of the bay with commentary (Golden Gate Bridge, Alcatraz, Sausalito)
Blue and Gold Fleet
→ Pier 39 and 41

Tel. 773 1188 / Price $60 (duration 8 hours) Cruise across the bay (Alcatraz, Sausalito) and coach excursions to the Wine Country, Carmel and Monterey.
By bike
Blazing Saddles (A F2)
→ 1095 Columbus Ave / Francisco St. Tel. 202 8888 From $20/day Explore the coastline, cross the Golden Gate Bridge, ride along the paths of the Golden Gate Park by bike.

GUIDED TOURS

Architecture
Victorian Home Walk
→ Leaves Westin St Francis Hotel (Union Square) daily at 11am. Tel. 252 9485 $20 (2 ½ hrs) Discover the treasures of Victorian architecture on foot.
Murals
Precita Eyes Mural

Arts Center
→ 2981 24th St / Harrison St Tel. 285 2287. Daily at 11am, 1.30pm; Sun 11pm. From $10 (1 ½ hrs) Marvel at the multicolored wall frescoes of the Latin American community in the Mission.
Gastronomy
Wok Wiz Chinatown Tours and Cooking Center
→ 654 Commercial St Tel. 981 8989 Daily 10am; $28 (without lunch); $40 (with lunch) Walking tour organized by chef Shirley Fong-Torre: architecture, traditional herbalists and culinary delights of Chinatown.
Californian wines
→ California Wine Tours Tel. 800 294 6386
→ Napa Valley Wine Tours Tel. 800 789 9575 Four- or eight-hour tours to discover and understand Californian wines. From $90–140 per person.

The shoreline from Fort Mason to Fisherman's Wharf bears witness to San Francisco's seafaring past with its restored ships anchored to the wooden quays. In the old fishing harbor, however, marine industries have given way to tourism, with gift shops and restaurants now occupying the former fish canneries. Overlooking the bustle of the port, Russian Hill (which takes its name from the belief that Russian seal hunters buried their dead here), offers stunning views of the bay from its steep shop-lined streets, which sometimes come to an end as stairways.

GREEN'S

RESTAURANTS

Mezes (A A4)
➔ *2373 Chestnut St / Divisadero St. Tel. 409 7111 Sun, Tue-Thu 5–9pm (10pm Fri-Sat). Closed bank hols*
A white Greek-style interior, a warm Mediterranean welcome and genuine Greek cooking: pork *souvlaki*, calamars with lemon; *dolmates* (vine leaves), *horitaki* (raw vegetables and feta). Wonderful selection of Greek wines. Terrace in summer.
À la carte $20–25.

Zarzuela (A E4)
➔ *2000 Hyde St / Union St Tel. 346 0800 Tue-Sat 5.30pm–10pm (10.30pm Fri-Sat) Closed Thanksgiving*
A short trip to the heart of the very best of Spanish cuisine: seafood *zarzuela*, gazpacho, paella or tapas. Sangria by the glass and fruity Rioja wines. À la carte $25–30.

Izzy's Steak & Chop House (A B3)
➔ *3345 Steiner St (between Chestnut and Lombard sts) Tel. 563 0488 / Mon-Sat 5.30–10pm (5pm Sun)*
A saloon-style steakhouse where the beef is king and served as a 16-oz New York Strip Steak (the

house specialty), steak *au poivre* (with cream and brandy), hamburger, blackened filet, T-bone... Very generous portions; simple but tasty side dishes (try the creamed spinach and Izzy's potatoes). À la carte $30.

Alioto's (A F2)
➔ *8 Fisherman's Wharf / Taylor St. Tel. 673 0183 Daily 11am–11pm*
Alioto's has been one of the highlights of Fisherman's Wharf since 1925. On the menu: super-fresh fish and seafood, prepared in a variety of styles, to savor in the beautiful room with wall seats on the 2nd floor, looking out on the bay. À la carte $35–40.

Green's (A C2)
➔ *Fort Mason Center, bldg A, Marina Blvd / Buchanan St Tel. 771 6222 Lunch: Tue-Sat noon–2.30pm (2.30pm Sat) / Brunch: Sun 10.30am–2pm / Dinner: Tue-Sat 5.30–9.30pm Closed bank hols*
The temple of Californian vegetarian cuisine, prepared with originality and inventiveness by chef Annie Somerville. All the dishes use fresh ingredients straight out of the organic farm of the Green Gulch Zen Center. The enormous dining-room provides a

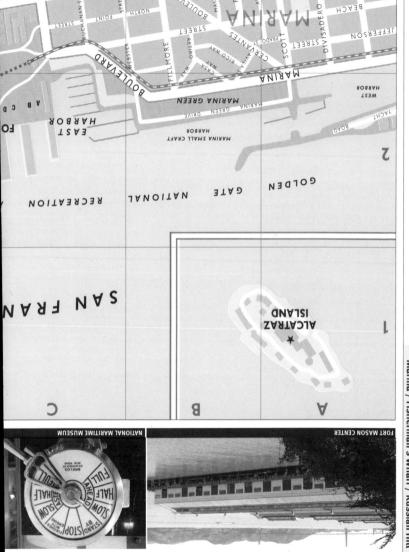

NATIONAL MARITIME MUSEUM

FORT MASON CENTER

LA

NORTH POINT ST.

CAPRA

PIERCE

AVILA

MALLORCA

BAY STREET

BUCHANAN STREET

NORTH POINT STREET

WEBSTER STREET

FILLMORE STREET

SCOTT STREET

CERVANTES

PRADO ST

RICO WAY

CASA WAY

RETIRO WAY

BOULEVARD

BEACH

JEFFERSON

DIVISADERO

3

MARINA

MARINA BOULEVARD

MARINA GREEN

MARINA GREEN DRIVE

EAST HARBOR

FORT

AB CD

WEST HARBOR

MARINA SMALL CRAFT HARBOR

YACHT ROAD

2

GOLDEN GATE NATIONAL RECREATION

SAN FRAN

SAN FRANCISCO

ALCATRAZ ISLAND

★

1

C

B

A

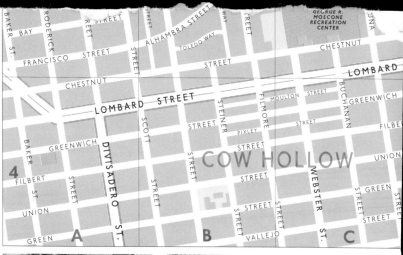

GEORGE R. MOSCONE RECREATION CENTER

BAKER ST. · BAY · RODERICK · STREET · STREET · ALHAMBRA STREET · WAY · TREET · CHESTNUT · LOMBARD

FRANCISCO · STREET · STREET · TOLEDO WAY · STREET

CHESTNUT · LOMBARD · STREET · STEINER · MOULTON STREET · BUCHANAN · GREENWICH

LOMBARD · STREET · STREET · FILMORE · STREET · FILBE

GREENWICH · DIVISADERO · STREET · SCOTT · STREET · PIXLEY · STREET · COW HOLLOW · UNION

4 · BAKER · FILBERT · ST. · STREET · STREET · STREET · WEBSTER · STREET · GREEN

UNION · ST. · STREET · STREET · STREET · GREEN

GREEN · **A** · **B** · VALLEJO · ST. · **C**

ALCATRAZ ISLAND

SAN FRANCISCO ART INSTITUTE

★ **Fort Mason Center**
(**A** C-D2)

→ *Beach St (between Laguna St and Marina Blvd) Tel. 441 3400*
Outstanding conversion of a vast complex of barracks and warehouses into one of the city's biggest art centers: theaters, cafés, restaurants, cultural associations and museums have taken over this beautiful space by the edge of the water.

Museum of Craft and Folk Arts (MOCFA)

→ *Tel. 775 0991. Tue-Fri, Sun 11am–5pm (10am Sat). Free Sat 10am–noon and 1st Wed of the month*
Popular arts and crafts from

all over the world.

Museo Italo-Americano

→ *Bldg C. Tel. 673 2200 Wed-Sun noon–5pm (free 1st Wed of month noon–7pm); closed bank hols*
Modern works by Italian or Italian-American artists.

African-American Historical & Cultural Society Museum

→ *Building C. Tel. 441 0640 Wed-Sun noon–5pm (free 1st Wed of the month); closed July 1–12*
Tributes to the outstanding figures of California's black community.

★ **National Maritime Museum** (**A** E2)

→ *900 Beach St / Polk St Tel. 556 3002. Daily 10am–*

5pm; closed bank hols. Free
Set in an old Art Deco casino (1939) done up like a steamship, this museum covers the city's entire naval history and displays models, old navigation instruments, paintings and photographs.

★ **Hyde Street Pier Historic Ships** (**A** E2)

→ *Hyde Street Pier Tel. 556 6435. Daily 9.30am–5.30pm (5pm in winter); closed bank hols*
Six magnificent ships, anchored off the old ferry terminal, are mementos of the city's naval glory in the 19th century. The stars are the steel-hulled three-masted *Baclutha* (1886),

the flagship of the US merchant fleet, and the impressive paddle steame *Eureka* (1890), that was in service until 1857.

★ **Fisherman's Wharf** (**A** F2)

→ *Between Jefferson, Beac Hyde and Taylor sts*
At the time of the goldrush the Italian immigrants, sic of mining, turned to fishin From the mid-19th century the city's fleet was based Fisherman's Wharf: every day the *felucas* unloaded crab, salmon and shrimp into the warehouses. The seafood restaurants and tourist malls have now replaced the canneries,

N · VNEL · INDIA BASIN · et

CABLE CARS

The most famous of all San Francisco's transport services, classified as a historic monument in 1964. Tickets are $2 one-way.

Daily 6am–1am
California line
→ From Market St to Van Ness Ave, via Nob Hill and Chinatown
Powell–Hyde line
→ From Powell / Market turntable to Aquatic Park, via Nob Hill and Russian Hill
Powell–Mason line
→ From Powell / Market turntable to Bay St at Fisherman's Wharf, via Nob Hill

CABLE CAR TURNTABLE

CITY LIGHTS BOOKSTORE

RESTAURANTS

Tax
Add 8.25% to the total price.
Tipping
Add 15–20% to the overall total of the bill.

SHOWS

Opera, ballet, classical music
Most of the venues are in the Civic Center (War Memorial Opera House, Davies Symphony Hall, Graham Auditorium).
War Memorial Opera House (D C4)
→ 301 Van Ness Ave /Grove St Tel. 864 3330 (box office)
www.sfopera.com
San Francisco Ballet (season Feb–May) and San Francisco Opera (season Sep–June).
Davies Symphony Hall (D C4)
→ 201 Van Ness Ave
Tel. 864 6000 (box office)
www.sfsymphony.org
Concerts by the S Francisco

Symphony Orchestra (season Sep-June).
Theaters
Concentrated in the Theater District (between Sutter, Powell, Geary and Taylor sts).
American Conservatory Theater (C B2)
→ 415 Geary St. Tel. 749 2228 http://act-sf.org/
Classical and contemporary repertoire.
Movie theaters
Movie Phone
→ Tel. 777 3456
www.moviefone.com
Programs and screening times of movie theaters in the Bay Area. Ticket sales service (by credit card, commission $1).
Embarcadero (B C5)
→ One Embarcadero Center (Sacramento and Battery sts) Tel. 352 0810
Blockbusters, foreign releases and garlic popcorn in a comfortable five-plex.
AMC Kabuki 8 (D A3)
→ Japan Center, 1881 Post

Street. Tel. 922 4262
Eight-screen complex in the heart of the Japan Center. Stages the San Francisco International Film Festival in April.
Information & bookings
San Francisco Bay Guardian and the San Francisco Weekly
→ Every Wed in cafés or newspaper distributors
The week's cultural and sportive events. Free.
Events Line
→ Recorded information, daily, 24 hrs. Tel. 391 2001
Details of cultural activities by telephone.
Western States Ticket Service
→ Tel. 800 326 0331
Ticket sales for major concerts, theater shows and sporting events.
Discounts
TIX Bay Area (C B2)
→ Tel. 433 7827
Union Square, on Powell St, between Geary and Post sts
Tue-Thu 11am–6pm (7pm

Fri-Sat); Sun 11am–3pm
www.theatrebayarea.org
50% off tickets for the same day. Payment in cash only.
Internet booking
www.ticketmaster.com
www.tickets.com

CALENDAR OF EVENTS

Late Jan/early February
Chinese New Year: big parade with golden dragon and fireworks in Chinatown's streets.
March
St Patrick's Day
(weekend near March 17)
Parades and beer drinking.
May
Cinco de Mayo
(weekend near May 5)
Commemoration of the Mexican victory over the French at the Battle of Puebla (1862). Dances and parades in the Mission.
Bay to Breakers
(Third Sun; from Embarcadero to Golden Gate Park)

J
S
a
J
In
Fir
be
Fish
Poll
Live
Cabl
Cham
Comp
bell-ri
cable
Squar
Septe
Folsom
(late Se
craziest
Octobe
Hallowe
Costume
dancing in
and clubs.

NEWSSTAND

Jogging in costume.
Carnival
(*Memorial Day weekend*)
Music, dancing and a big
carnival in the Mission.

une
itreet fairs in North Beach
nd Haight St.

uly
ndependence Day (*July 4*)
eworks over the bay,
st seen from
herman's Wharf.
k Street Fair (*mid-July*)
music and markets.
e Car Bell-Ringing
npionship (*mid-July*)
etition for the best
nger among the
car drivers (in Union
e).

mber
Street Fair
p) The city's
street fair.

n (*Oct 31*)
music and
the streets, bars

November
Dia de los Muertos (*Nov 2*)
Celebration of the Mexican
Day of the Dead in the
streets of the Mission.

TELEPHONE

UK / San Francisco
Dial 00 + 1 + 415
+ 7-figure number
San Francisco / UK
Dial 011 + 44 + number
(without the first o)
Useful numbers
San Francisco Visitor
Information Center
→ *900 Market St / Powell St,
Hallidie Plaza (underground)*
Tel. 391 2000 (24-hr info)
*Mon-Fri 8.30am–5pm;
Sat 9am–3pm (2pm Sun)*
Tourist information and
sale of City Pass cards.
Lost and Found
→ Tel. 923 6168
Objects found on the
public transport services.
UK embassy
→ Tel. 617 1300

www.britsinthestates.com
Emergencies
Police, firefighters
→ Tel. 911

INTERNET

San Francisco online
→ *wwwsfgate.com*
Website of the San
Francisco Chronicle:
cultural events, daily life,
weather etc.
→ *sfbay.yahoo.com*
Event calendar and
selection of restaurants.
→ *www.sfbayconcerts.com*
Internet café
Quetzal Café (**D** C2)
→ *1234 Polk St / Sutter St*
Tel. 673 4181 / Mon-Fri
6am–11pm; (7am Sat-Sun)
Macs and PCs. Café.
Weblightning Café (**D** C2)
→ *Pier 39, Bldg P, Bush St.*
Tel. 397 0898 /
Daily 9am–8pm
The fastest connection
the city; possible digital
film downloads onto CDs.

A NOUVELLE PÂTISSERIE

BLACK HORSE LONDON PUB

FUMIKI

beautiful panoramic view of the Golden Gate Bridge. Take out available. À la carte $50.

CAFÉS, PATISSERIE

Buena Vista Café (A E2)
→ 2765 Hyde St / Beach St
Tel. 474 5044 / Sun-Fri 9am–2am; Sat-Sun 8am–2am
Ever since 1952 the Buena Vista Café has been packing in customers eager to try the house specialty: Irish coffee (some 2,000 are served each day). Sit in the lovely old-fashioned lounge and watch the boats pass by. Dish of the day, snacks. Irish Coffee $5.50.

Coffee Roastery (A B4)
→ 2191 Union St / Fillmore St. Tel. 922 9559
Daily 6am–10pm
A treat for coffee lovers! More than 30 freshly milled varieties (Kenyan, Tanzanian, Jamaican, Guatemalan), sold in packets or drunk on the premises, in the big armchairs made from the canvas used for coffee sacks.

La Nouvelle Pâtisserie (A C4)
→ 2184 Union St / Fillmore St
Tel. 931 7655
Sun-Fri 7am–8pm;
Sat 8am–11pm

This elegant French-owned patisserie, with all the style of a chic bistro, has been selling delicious pastries for over 20 years. On display: fruit tarts, macaroons, petits fours. Take out or eat on the spot, in the beautiful tiled dining-room.

BARS

Balboa Café (A B4)
→ 3199 Fillmore St / Greenwich St
Tel. 921 3944
Mon-Fri 11.30am–2am; Sat-Sun 10am–2am
Enjoy the best cocktails in town in a delightful, perfectly restored 1930s setting. From $5. Excellent hamburgers at lunchtime.

Black Horse London Deli (A D4)
→ 1514 Union St / Van Ness Ave. Tel. 928 2414
Mon-Fri noon–midnight;
Sat-Sun 4pm–midnight
The smallest bar in the city. This tiny British-style pub is complete with wooden shelves and the inevitable dart-board. English beer and imported cheeses .

Bus Stop (A C4)
→ 1901 Union St /
Laguna St. Tel. 567 6905
Daily 9am–2am
The doyen of San

Francisco's sports bars has been playing host to all types of fans ever since its founding in 1900. The program includes screenings of major events, bottled and draft beer, and guaranteed atmosphere.

SHOPPING

Bebe (A C4)
→ 2095 Union St /
Webster St. Tel. 563 2323
Mon-Sat 10am–8pm;
Sun 11am–6pm
The headquarters of this trendy Californian chain. Colorful little tops, jeans, trousers, shirts.
For adolescents and young women.

Fumiki (A C4)
→ 2001 Union St /
Buchanan St. Tel. 922 0573
Mon-Sat 10am–6pm;
Sun noon–5pm
Exquisite Japanese refinement applied to furniture, pottery and decoration in a huge store set off by Zen-style fountains. Marvelous, but pricey too.

Ghirardelli's Chocolate Manufactory (A E2)
→ 900 North Point St /
Larkin St, Clock Tower Bldg,
1st floor. Tel. 474 3938
Daily 9.30am–11.30pm
(midnight Fri-Sat)

Domingo Ghirardelli's striking redbrick factory, now converted into a shopping mall, still houses its most famous chocolate shop/tearoom. On display in the small store are chocolate-coated almonds and hazelnuts, sample bars, various combinations (cookies and creams, plain chocolate and raspberries) and beautiful packages in the form of a cable car; and a soda-fountain for ice-cream soda fans.

The Basic Brown Bear Factory (A E2)
→ The Cannery Shopping Center, 2801 Leavenworth St / Beach St. Tel. 931 6670
Mon-Sat 10am–6pm; Sun 11am–6pm. Guided tours daily 1pm (11am Sat)
From the 10-feet high 'Big Fred' to 'Baby', you will find all imaginable soft bears here. Guided tour of the factory with possibility of making your own Teddy Bear. Ask the store for details.

Real Food Company (A B4)
→ 3060 Fillmore St /
Filbert St. Tel. 567 6900
Daily 8am–9pm
Wonderful, classy grocer's store replete with mouthwatering delicacies: salads, cheeses, sausages and a wide range of Californian wines.

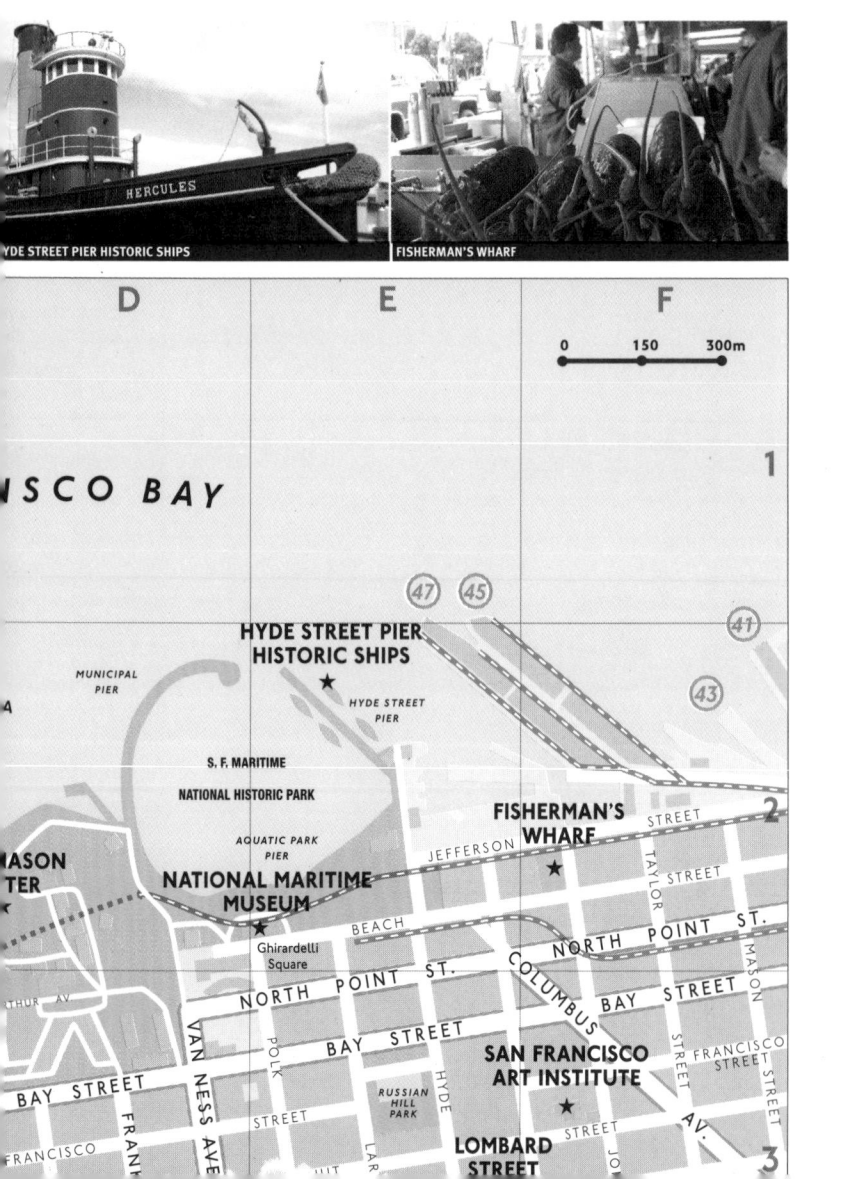

HYDE STREET PIER HISTORIC SHIPS

FISHERMAN'S WHARF

D

E

F

0   150   300m

1

ISCO BAY

47   45

41

HYDE STREET PIER
HISTORIC SHIPS
★
HYDE STREET
PIER

43

MUNICIPAL
PIER

S. F. MARITIME

NATIONAL HISTORIC PARK

AQUATIC PARK
PIER

FISHERMAN'S
WHARF
★

JEFFERSON   STREET

TAYLOR   STREET

2

MASON
TER
★

NATIONAL MARITIME
MUSEUM
★
Ghirardelli
Square

BEACH

NORTH   POINT   ST.

MASON   STREET

THUR   AV

NORTH   POINT   ST.

COLUMBUS

BAY   STREET

FRANCISCO
STREET

BAY   STREET

VAN   NESS   AVE.

POLK   STREET

BAY   STREET

RUSSIAN
HILL
PARK

HYDE   STREET

SAN FRANCISCO
ART INSTITUTE
★

STREET

AV.

FRANCISCO

FRAN

LOMBARD
STREET

3

CHESTNUT STREET
LOMBARD STREET
GREENWICH STREET
FILBERT STREET
UNION STREET
GREEN STREET
VALLEJO STREET
BROADWAY
PACIFIC AVENUE
JACKSON ST.

LEAVENWORTH STREET
TAYLOR

NORTH BEACH

RUSSIAN HILL

OCTAGON HOUSE ★

VAN NESS AVENUE

COOLBRITH PARK

4

D   E   F

ROADWAY

LOMBARD STREET

OCTAGON HOUSE

ut the port has not lost its harm. Little fishing boats an still be seen to and fro cross the bay every day.

★ Alcatraz Island (A A1)
→ Ferries Blue & Gold Fleet, ier 41 Tel. 705 5555 www.blueandgoldfleet.com aily 9.30am–4.15pm .15pm Sep–March). Book at east a week ahead in season his bleak little island, once nly inhabited by birds lcatraz means pelican in panish), was the world's ost famous prison from 934 until its closure in 963. Separated from the ainland by 1 ½ miles of old and dangerous seas, played host to the most

hardened criminal. The isolation of the prisoners, the huge number of guards and the invulnerable security system, made escaping impossible, even for its most famous inmate, Al Capone!

★ San Francisco Art Institute (A F3)
→ 800 Chestnut St (between Jones and Leavenworth sts) Tel. 771 7020 / Walter & McBean Galleries: Mon-Sat 11am–6pm; Diego Rivera Gallery: Mon-Sat 8am–9pm Discover the painters and sculptors of tomorrow in this prestigious art school, founded in 1871. There are temporary exhibitions of

works by the most promising students in the two galleries in this fine Spanish neo-Colonial building.

★ Octagon House (A D4)
→ 2645 Gough St / Union St Tel. 441 7512. Visits on 2nd Sun, 2nd and 4th Thu of each month: noon–3pm (except Jan and bank hols). Free
In his essay A Home For All (1848), the nephrologist O. Fowler imagined an octagonal house that would provide its occupants with light, heat and comfort. In 1861 the architect McElroy made the dream a reality by building an astonishing 8-sided building perforated

with openings that allowed the light to penetrate into all the rooms. It is now a museum of furniture and decorative arts from the Colonial and Federal periods.

★ Lombard Street (A E3)
Lombard St (between Hyde and Leavenworth sts)
In 1928 the City Hall developed Lombard Street in order to make Russian Hill accessible to cars. Its 27% gradient and its eight formidable hairpin curves flanked by banks of hydrangeas have earned it the nickname 'Crookedest Street in the world.' It is well-known for featuring in a number of TV ads.

JACKSON SQUARE

TRANSAMERICA PYRAMID

← Map D

← Map C

STREET

VALLEJO STREET

BROADWAY

KEROUAC ALLEY

PACIFIC

AVENUE

PACIFIC

JACKSON

STREET

CABLE CAR BARN MUSEUM

OLD CHINESE TELEPHONE EXCHANGE ★

TRAN P

CHINESE HOSPITAL

PORTSMOUTH SQUARE

WASHINGTON

5 NOB HILL

CHINATOWN

STREET

COMMERCIAL

CLAY

OLD SAINT MARY'S CHURCH ★

GRACE CATHEDRAL

SACRAMENTO

CALIFORNIA

KEARNY STREET

GRANT

BANK AMER

STREET

PINE

LEAVENWORTH STREET

JONES

TAYLOR

MASON

POWELL

STREET

CHINATOWN GATE ★

STREET

BUSH

STOCKTON

STREET

SUTTER

MONTG

STREET

POST

Union Square

MAIDEN LN

STREET

6

A

GEARY

B

★ **Coit Tower** (**B** B3)
→ *Telegraph Hill Blvd*
Tel. 362 0808
April-Sep: daily 10am– 7pm
(6pm Oct-March)
At the top of Telegraph Hill, a strange fluted tower (1934) in the form of a fire hose commemorates the admiration of an eccentric widow (Lillie Hitchcock Coit) for her city's firemen. There are frescoes illustrating life at the time of the Great Crash of 1929 in the lobby and breathtaking views of North Beach and the bay from the top.

★ **Filbert steps** (**B** B3)
Take a pastoral stroll in the heart of the city. Filbert

Street changes into steps from the top of Telegraph Hill and heads down toward Levi Plaza and the Embarcadero, passing the lush gardens of 19th-century wooden villas, ablaze with fuchsias and bougainvillea.

★ **Washington Square** (**B** A4)
Green lifeblood of North Beach, the stronghold of the city's Italian community. On the grass amateur painters rub shoulders with Tai Chi adepts and pensioners. To the west of the park (1862), a pentagonal area planted with cypresses, cedars and

sycamores sets off the white St Peter and St Paul Church (1924). A symbol of the neighborhood's recent multiculturalism, masses are said here in English, Italian and Cantonese.

★ **Jackson Square** (**B** B4)
Cross a street and go back to the 19th century. Poised between North Beach and the Financial District, Jackson Square still sports its redbrick and stucco buildings, in sharp contrast to the adjoining skyscrapers. Nowadays lawyers and antique dealers have bought up the old houses in Barbary Coast, a neighborhood that acquired

notoriety in the Gold Rush.
★ **Transamerica Pyramid** (**B** C5)
→ *600 Montgomery St / Merchant St*
This monumental tower (1972) is to San Francisco what the Empire State Building is to New York. A pyramidal obelisk 853-ft high made of earthquake-proof concrete and steel, a strange mixture of architectural references to ancient Egypt and hi-tech materials. Visitors aren't admitted to the building anymore but thanks to video cameras placed on the rooftop you can still enjoy dizzying views

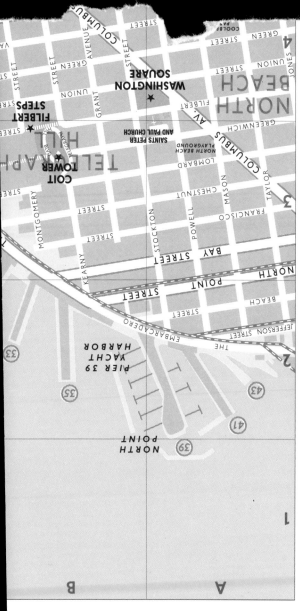

COLUMBUS STREET

GREEN STREET

COOLEY PA?

WASHINGTON SQUARE

NORTH BEACH

FILBERT

UNION STREET

JONES STREET

GREENWICH AV.

COLUMBUS AV.

SAINTS PETER AND PAUL CHURCH

NORTH BEACH PLAYGROUND

LOMBARD

FILBERT STEPS

TELEGRAPH HILL

COIT TOWER

TELEGRAPH HILL

CHESTNUT

FRANCISCO

TAYLOR

MASON

POWELL

STOCKTON

MONTGOMERY

KEARNY

STREET

BAY STREET

NORTH POINT STREET

BEACH STREET

JEFFERSON STREET

THE EMBARCADERO

PIER 39 YACHT HARBOR

NORTH POINT

WASHINGTON SQUARE

FILBERT STEPS

COIT TOWER

North Beach / Financial District / Chinatown

The slopes of Telegraph Hill are marked by precipitous cliffs and wooden houses with exuberant gardens. At its foot, North Beach, the Little Italy of San Francisco, with an almost Mediterranean climate, boasts countless European cafés and delicatessens in a non-stop hubbub. Montgomery Street cuts through the cluster of skyscrapers that makes up Downtown and the Financial District. This area also borders on Chinatown: Asian San Francisco unfurls around Grant Avenue in a flurry of exotic fruit stalls, Chinese restaurants and traditional herbalists.

FIOR D'ITALIA   PIPERADE

RESTAURANTS

Fior d'Italia (B B4)
→ *601 Union St / Stockton St Tel. 986 1886*
Daily 11.30am–10.30pm
A North Beach institution that will soon proudly boast 120 years of existence. The menu is amazingly varied: osso buco and polenta, fried squid, gnocchi, risotto, saltimbocca, pasta, etc. Simple but stylish dining-room looking out on Washington Square Park. Dishes $13–27.

Tadich Grill (B B6)
→ *240 California St (between Front and Battery sts) Tel. 391 1849*
Mon–Fri 11am–9.30pm; Sat 11.30am–9.30pm
Another San Francisco institution. Founded in 1849 by Croatian immigrants, Tadich is the oldest California restaurant in continuous operation. Other than seafood, it serves excellent pork loin, hamburgers and salads. $12–25.

New Kan's Restaurant (B B5)
→ *708 Grant Ave / Sacramento St Tel. 982 2388*
Daily 10.30am–10pm
In the heart of Chinatown, a traditional Chinese restaurant specializing in seafood and Peking duck. The opulent, if slightly dated, dining-rooms, look out on the ceaseless bustle of Grant Avenue.
À la carte $15.

Aqua (B C5)
→ *252 California St (Battery and Front sts) Tel. 956 9662*
Lunch: Mon–Fri 11.30am–2.30pm / Dinner: Mon–Sun 5.30–10.30pm
This formal dining-room serves innovative seafood dishes created by chef Michael Mina. Its high ceilings, beautiful art, and huge flower arrangements ($150,000 is budgeted for them annually) complement the food. Menu options include medallions of Ahi tuna and petrale sole. Dishes $11–55.

Café Jacqueline (B B4)
→ *1454 Grant Ave / Union St Tel. 981 5565*
Wed–Sun 5.30pm–11pm; closed bank hols
Soufflés in a variety of flavors (seafood, Gruyère and broccoli, chocolate and Grand Marnier), in an elegant room ideal for romantic dinners. $25–50 per soufflé (for two).

Piperade (B C4)
→ *1015 Battery St / Union St Tel. 391 2555 Lunch: Mon–Fri 11.30am–3pm. Dinner: Mon–*

SCA

BANANA REPUBLIC

CITY LIGHTS BOOKSTORE

Sat 5.30pm–10.30pm
Closed Christmas, Jan 1
Chef Gerald Hirigoyen has chosen a huge dockside warehouse to create a restaurant inspired by the Old World. His cooking balances tradition and innovation, with Basque and Mediterranean touches: mussels in Pastis, *poulet basquaise*... À la carte $35.

TEAROOM

Imperial Tea Court (B A4)
→ *1411 Powell St (between Broadway and Vallejo St) Tel. 788 6080*
Wed-Mon 11am–6.30pm
Chrysanthemum, Lapsang Souchong, pine needle... this authentic Chinese tea house explores all the fragrances of the ancestral brew. Roy Fong, the owner, helps novices make their choice.

BARS, CLUBS, CONCERT VENUES

Bubble Lounge (B C5)
→ *714 Montgomery St / Washington St. Tel. 434 4204*
Mon 4.30pm–midnight (1am Tue-Thu; 2am Fri); Sat 5.30pm–2am
A must for champagne lovers. Over 30 vintages, served by the glass or by

the bottle. Test samples for lower budgets. Smart dress required.

Harry Denton's Starlight Room (B B6)
→ *Sir Francis Drake Hotel, 450 Powell St (between Post and Sutter sts) Tel. 395 8595*
Daily 6pm–2am
Dive into the heart of chic San Francisco nightlife. One of the most select bar-restaurants in town, this elegant space is perched on the 21st floor of the Sir Francis Drake Hotel. Live music duing the week, DJs at the week-end. Strong drinks and a spectacular view of the city lights.

Specs' Twelve Adler Museum Café (B B4)
→ *Columbus Ave/Broadway Tel. 421 4112*
Daily 5pm–2am
This dark fisherman's den filled with maritime odds and ends and postcards has been, since the 1940s, a meeting place for Beat poets, dockers and musicians. Blues and jazz in the background.

Tosca Café (B B4)
→ *242 Columbus Ave (between Broadway and Pacific Ave) Tel. 986 9651*
Daily 5pm–2am (midnight Mon; 1am tue-Thu); closed bank hols
With photos of tenors and

divas on the walls, a jukebox with the great operatic arias, this dark café is where opera lovers and movie stars meet (Francis Ford Coppola allegedly wrote the script of *The Godfather* here). The house cappuccino is a mixture of milk, hot chocolate and brandy.

The Saloon (B B4)
→ *1232 Grant Ave / Vallejo St. Tel. 989 7666*
Daily noon–2am
This is the city's oldest bar, dating back to the Gold Rush days. It is also the best blues bar in San Francisco – some say the world – and as such, a favorite spot among North Beach locals in the know. Daily concerts 9.30pm (plus 4.30 Fri-Sun).

SHOPPING

Banana Republic (B B6)
→ *256 Grant Ave / Sutter St Tel. 788 3087*
Mon-Sat 10am–8pm; Sun 11am–7pm
Stylish clothes at this San Francisco-based chain.

City Lights Bookstore (B B4)
→ *261 Columbus Ave / Broadway. Tel. 362 8193*
Daily 10am–midnight
The most emblematic bookstore in town,

founded by Lawrence Ferlinghetti, poet and leading light of the Beat Generation. Radical posters on the walls, wonderful choice of foreign literature and impressive poetry section upstairs.

Discount Camera (B B6)
→ *33 Kearny St / Market St Tel. 392 1100*
Mon-Sat 8.30am–6.30pm; Sun 9.30am–6pm
All the leading brands (Canon, Nikon, Pentax, Minolta, etc.) of photographic material at discount prices.

Molinari Delicatessen (B B4)
→ *373 Columbus Ave / Vallejo St. Tel 421 2337*
Mon-Fri 8am–6pm; Sat 7.30am–5.30pm
Cheeses, hams, cooked dishes, cakes, wines... all the Italian products required for a picnic in Washington Square Park. Sandwiches to take out.

Shoe Pavilion (B C5)
→ *351 California St (Sansom and Battery sts) Tel. 362 8593*
Mon-Fri 9am–7pm; Sat 10am–6pm
Everything from classic loafers to trainers for men and women. Shoes from top brands (Massimo, Nike, Timberland, Esprit, Nine West) with up to 60% discount.

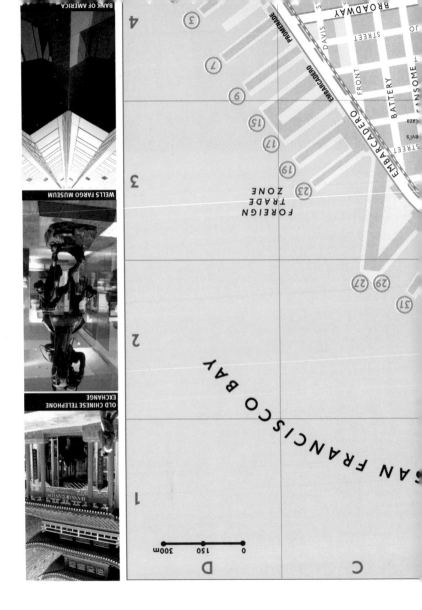

BANK OF AMERICA

WELLS FARGO MUSEUM

OLD CHINESE TELEPHONE
EXCHANGE

BROADWAY

DAVIS STREET JO

FRONT STREET

BATTERY STREET

SANSOME

Plaza

Levi's

STREET

EMBARCADERO

PROMENADE

EMBARCADERO

FOREIGN
TRADE
ZONE

SAN FRANCISCO BAY

③

⑦

⑨

⑮

⑰

⑲

㉓

㉗ ㉙

㉛

4

3

2

1

D

C

300m 150 0

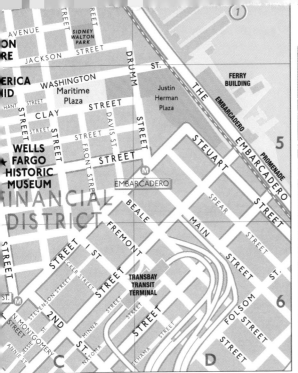

OLD ST MARY'S CHURCH

CHINATOWN GATE

Map C →

the city from the Virtual
servation Desk, at the
ot of the building.

**Old Chinese Telephone
change (B** B5)
→ *Bank of Canton,
ashington St / Grant Ave*
reen tiles, a red-pillared
cade, curving roofs:
is building boasts all
e attributes of a genuine
goda. The foremost
ample of Chinese
chitecture in San
ancisco once housed
e Pacific Telephone and
elegraph Company.
astery of five different
ninese dialects was an
dispensable requirement
r the switchboard

operators.
**★ Wells Fargo History
Museum (B** C5)
→ *420 Montgomery St /
California St. Tel. 396 2619
Mon-Fri 9am–5pm. Free*
Travel through time to the
days of the Gold Rush,
and pay homage to Wells
Fargo and Co., whose
stagecoaches loaded
with gold and bank bills
connected the Pacific with
the Atlantic. There are some
exhibits featuring Black
Bart, a Californian Robin
Hood famous for holding
up stagecoaches.
★ Bank of America (B B5)
→ *California St / Kearny St*
Classic example of 1970s

architecture, this enormous
780-ft tower dominates the
skyline of the Financial
District. At dusk, the plated
red granite slabs on the
52-floor façade take on a
golden hue, visible from
miles away.
**★ Old St Mary's
Church (B** B5)
→ *660 California St /
Grant Ave. Tel. 288 3800
Daily 7.30am–4.30pm*
The neo-Gothic redbrick
lines of the city's first
cathedral (1854) emerge
incongruously above the
souvenir shops and fast-
food joints, a striking relic
of the extravagance of the
Gold Rush. Under the

chiming clock, a stern
quotation from Ecclesiastes
admonished the customers
of the nearby brothels:
'My son, manage time and
avoid evil.'
★Chinatown Gate (B B6)
→ *Grant Ave / Bush St*
Pass through this large
gateway (1970), inspired
by traditional pagodas, to
enter the second largest
Chinese community
outside Asia. Two stone
lions watch over the green-
tiled triple gate that leads
onto the bustle of Grant
Avenue, studded with
Chinese restaurants,
souvenir shops and
antiquarians.

MC ALLISTER STREET

SIAN ART FONDATION

SAN FRANCISCO PUBLIC LIBRARY

Ⓜ CIVIC CENTER

YERBA BUENA CENTER FOR THE ARTS

CARTOON ART MUSEUM

★ Ferry Building (C E1)
→ Embarcadero Promenade / Market St

Up until 1936 the harbor station was the focal point of this bustling city. The enormous building was built in 1896 to accommodate the 100,000 ferryboat commuters who descended upon San Francisco every day. Its central hall, made of Colusa sandstone, is adjoined by a monumental 235-ft tower inspired by the Giralda cathedral in Seville, Spain. Today few ferries still disembark here, but the tower's four clocks are still in perfect working order.

★ Embarcadero Promenade (C E1)

From Fisherman's Wharf to China Basin, the old harbor is endowed with a spectacular promenade stretching for three miles along the seafront, offering stunning views across the east of the bay and, inland, dazzling tricks of perspective with the skyscrapers of the Financial District. In 1996, the road was named Herb Caen Way in homage to the city's most famous gossip columnist.

★ SF-Oakland Bay Bridge (C F1)

The longest suspended steel bridge in the world.

Finished in 1936, a masterpiece of elegance and simplicity 8½ miles long, it links San Francisco and the east bay via Yerba Buena Island. The bridge is out of bounds for pedestrians, but it can always be admired from the city's high points.

★ Union Square (C B2)

It was on this famous spot that the local population rallied the Union troops at the height of the American Civil War. Today, shopping complexes and fashion shops hug the edges of this vast palm-studded square, under the benevolent gaze of the Dewey Monument

(1901), a bronze statue s on the top of a Corinthian column to mark the American victory over Sp in Manila at the end of th 19th century. To the west, the three towers of the luxurious Westin Saint Francis Hotel dwarf the o buildings: the rosewood clock in its lobby is one o the favorite meeting plac for locals.

★ SFMoMa (C C2)
→ 151 3rd St / Minna St
Tel. 357 4000 / Mon-Tue, F
Sun 11am–6pm (9pm Thu)
free 1st Tue of month

Eclectic overview of desi sculpture, photography, architecture and

MOSCONE
CENTER

★ MOSCONE
CENTER

★ OLD UNITED STATES
MINT

★ YERBA BUENA CENTER
FOR THE ARTS

★ SFMOMA

★ CARTOON ART
MUSEUM

UNION
SQUARE

CHINATOWN
GATE

BANK OF
AMERICA

WELLS FARGO
MUSEUM

CALIFORNIA

FINANCIAL
DISTRICT

TRANSAMERICA
PYRAMID

OLD SAINT
MARY'S CHURCH

CHINATOWN

NOB HILL

CHINESE
HOSPITAL

OLD CHINESE
TELEPHONE
EXCHANGE

CABLE CAR
BARN MUSEUM

PORTSMOUTH
SQUARE

Haulde
Plaza

Embarcadero
Promenade

SF-OAKLAND BAY BRIDGE

EMBARCADERO PROMENADE

FERRY BUILDING

The Financial District is adjacent to the bay, bordered by the Embarcadero Promenade, a magnificent road with wide sidewalks perfect for running and roller blading. Once it passes the Andalusian forms of the Ferry Building, the huge steel supports of the Bay Bridge come into view. Market Street, flanked by shopping malls and sportswear stores, crosses the city from east to west: to the north are palm trees and shops on Union Square, the biggest concentration of trendy stores in town. To the south, SoMa (South of Market), once a working-class neighborhood, now the city's artistic and multimedia hotspot.

SOUTH PARK CAFÉ   LULU

RESTAURANTS

Farallon (**C** B2)
→ 450 Post St (between Mason and Powell sts)
Tel. 956 6969
Lunch: Tue-Sat 11.30am–2pm / Dinner: Mon-Sun 5.30–10.30pm
With décor designed to create the feel of an underwater fantasy, and a delicious menu, Farallon is a must. Lunch might include red wine-braised lamb shank, while dinner might start with caviar. There's also pan-roasted Alaskan halibut and hand-cut pasta, among many gourmet options. Dishes $30.

Fifth Floor (**C** B3)
→ 12 4th St / Market St (in the Hotel Palomar)
Tel. 348 1555
Breakfast: Mon-Fri 7–10am; Sat-Sun 8–11am / Dinner: Mon-Thu 5.30–10pm (11pm Fri-Sat)
Fifth Floor is stunningly decorated, managing to be both elegant and trendy. The menu is extensive, featuring French-style preparation of lobster, skate wing, crab and avocado pork belly. The prices are a little steep, but in this case you get what you pay for. Reservations are recommended, but you can always eat at the bar. Dishes from $31; $95 for the six-course gourmet menu.

South Park Café (**C** D3)
→ 108 South Park Ave (between 2nd, 3rd, Bryant, Brannan sts)
Tel. 495 7275 Mon-Sat 5.30–10pm
In the heartland of the multimedia industry, a restaurant inspired by a Parisian bistro, in both the decoration and the menu: mussels in white wine, breast of duck sautéed in honey sauce, brandade of cod. For dessert: the best chocolate profiteroles in San Francisco. The jazzy musical atmosphere at nights makes for relaxed dining. À la carte $35–40.

Lulu (**C** C3)
→ 816 Folsom St (between 4th and 5th sts) Tel. 495 5775
Daily 11.30am–3pm, 5.30–10.30pm
California is just one step away from Provence... at least chez Lulu, where Californian stylishness is applied to traditional Mediterranean cooking. Chicken grilled with herbs, pizzas, pasta, polenta with mushrooms, all served in a huge yellow and ocher dining-room.
À la carte $50.

SCUITS AND BLUES   NEIMAN MARCUS   URBAN OUTFITTERS

Postrio (C A2)

→ 545 Post St (between
Taylor and Mason sts)
Tel. 776 7825 Breakfast:
Mon–Fri 7–10am / Lunch:
Mon–Sat 11.30am–2pm /
Dinner: Sun–Wed 5.30–
10pm (10.30pm Thu–Sat)
With Wolfgang Puck as
executive chef, you really
can't go wrong. Postrio
serves food prepared
with Californian, Asian,
and Mediterranean
influences, emphasizing
fresh local produce.
Salmon is smoked in-
house, and meats are
prepared in an on-site
butcher shop. Dishes $55.

CAFÉ

Brainwash (C B4)

→ 1122 Folsom St
(between 7th and 8th sts)
Tel. 431-WASH
Sun–Thu 7am–11pm
(midnight Fri–Sat)
A space resembling an
artist's loft (large bay
windows, wood and
chrome furniture, exposed
beams, funk or jungle in
the background, some
times as live concerts) for
a dual-purpose venue:
café and laundromat.
Salads, soups, assorted
sandwiches and fish and
chips. Internet access.
Unequivocally cool.

BARS, NIGHTCLUBS, CONCERT VENUES

111 Minna (C C2)

→ 111 Minna St (between
Mission, Howard, 2nd and
New Montgomery sts)
Tel. 974 1719
Gallery: Mon–Fri noon–5pm;
Sat–Sun by appointment.
Club: 9 or 10pm–am
An art gallery by day,
a bar-club by night,
111 Minna is the epitome
of San Francisco chic.
Always jam-packed and
full of atmosphere.
Cover charge $5-10.

The Endup (C C4)

→ 401 6th St / Harrison St
Tel. 357 0827
Thu 10.30pm–4am (6am
Fri-Sat); Sat 10pm–4am;
Sun 6am–3am
The attractive courtyard
and bar is a haven for the
most assiduous night owls
after the city's bars have
closed. Dance the night
away to the sounds of
San Francisco's best DJs.

Biscuits and Blues (C B2)

→ 401 Mason St / Geary St
Tel. 292 2583
Daily 5pm–midnight
Or the New Orleans of San
Francisco. On the program
of this renowned music
club: delicious Southern
cooking (catfish, grilled
shrimps) and blues bands,

either local or from other
parts of the US.

Ten 15 (C B4)

→ 1015 Folsom St / 6th St
Tel. 431 1200 / Fri-Sat
10pm– 7am (5.30am Sun)
With six bars, three floors
and parties that often go
until dawn, this club is a
hub for San Francisco's
dance scene. World-class
DJs; extravagant lighting;
mainly dance, house and
techno music, more
experimental acts at the
week ends. Bring some
cash as drinks are not
cheap.

Warfield (C B3)

→ 982 Market St / 5th St
Tel. 775 7722
Doors open at 7pm,
concerts start 8pm
The most elegant rock
venue in town, built in
1922. Wonderful baroque
interior with ornate circles,
three bars, and a varied
program to suit all tastes
and ages.

SHOPPING

Neiman Marcus (C B2)

→ 150 Stockton St/Geary St
Tel. 362 3900
Mon–Sat 10am–7pm (8pm
Thu); Sun noon–6pm
This department store
wins all the prizes for
elegance. Its magnificent
atrium, decorated with

golden wood trim, towers
over the selection of
cosmetics, jewelry and
clothes, for men and
women. Luxury items,
and prices to match.

Urban Outfitters (C B3)

→ 80 Powell St / Market St
Tel. 989 1515
Mon–Sat 9.30am–7.30pm
(9pm Sun)
Jeans, sweatshirts, bags,
printed T-shirts and all
the other trappings needed
to keep up with the latest
street styles. Also, a wealth
of gadgets and kitsch
accessories for the home.

Old Navy (C B2)

→ 801 Market St / 4th St
Tel. 344 0375
Mon–Sat 9.30am–9pm;
Sun 11am–8pm
Old Navy has created a
casual, sporting look for the
entire family at prices that
cannot be matched
elsewhere: pants, shirts,
shorts, leather jackets,
dresses in a host of styles
and colors. Do not miss the
remnants on offer in the
basement, a real Mecca for
bargain hunters.

Jeremy's (C E3)

→ 2 South Park / 2nd St
Tel. 882 4929 / Mon-Sat
11am–6pm (5pm Sun)
The biggest names in
international fashion (Dolce
e Gabbana, Chanel, Prada)
at discount prices.

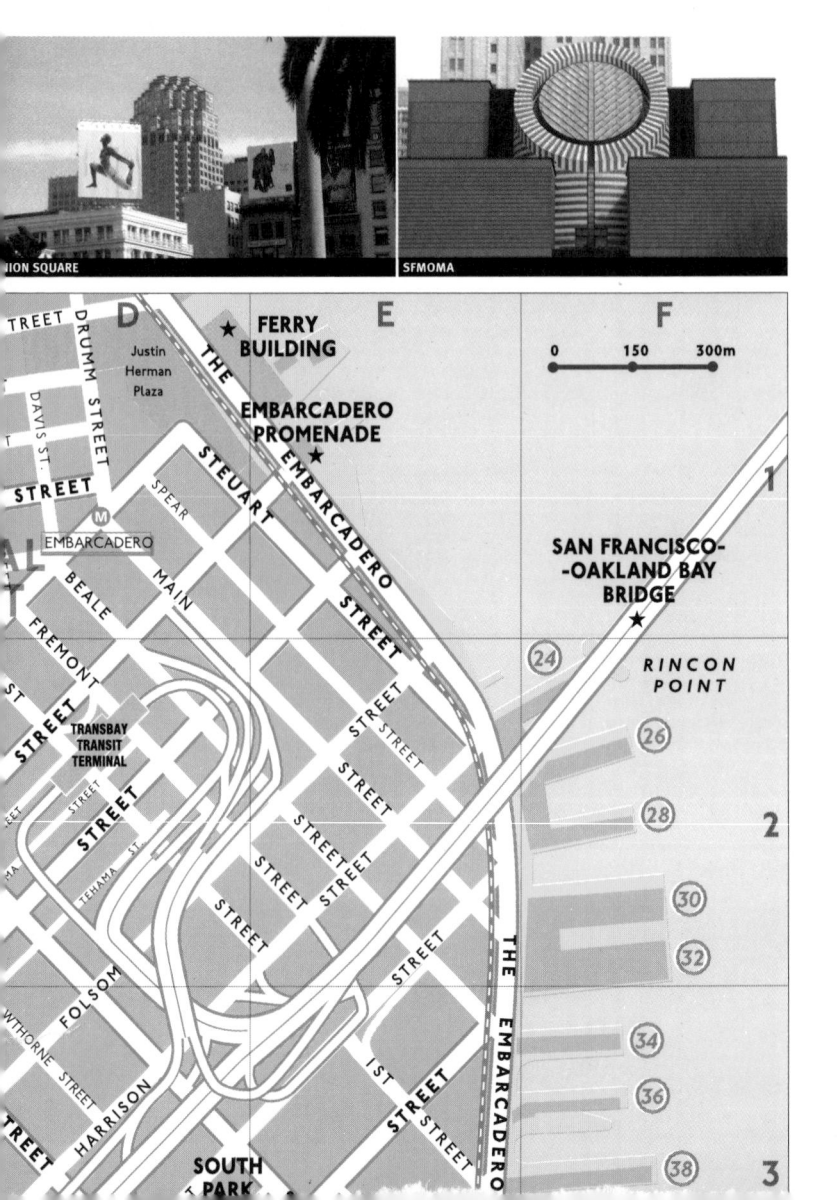

ION SQUARE

SFMOMA

D

E

F

★ **FERRY BUILDING**

Justin Herman Plaza

EMBARCADERO PROMENADE ★

0   150   300m

DRUMM STREET

DAVIS ST.

STREET

SPEAR

STEUART

THE EMBARCADERO

STREET

Ⓜ EMBARCADERO

BEALE

MAIN

SAN FRANCISCO- -OAKLAND BAY BRIDGE ★

FREMONT

1

Ⓐ24

RINCON POINT

TRANSBAY TRANSIT TERMINAL

STREET

STREET

STREET

Ⓐ26

STREET

STREET

Ⓐ28

STREET STREET

TEHAMA ST.

STREET STREET

STREET

Ⓐ30

Ⓐ32

2

FOLSOM

STREET

THE EMBARCADERO

Ⓐ34

WTHORNE STREET

HARRISON

Ⓐ36

TREET

1ST STREET

STREET

SOUTH PARK

Ⓐ38

3

OLD UNITED STATES MINT

SOUTH PARK

ntemporary art from
atisse to Warhol in a
ilding designed in 1955 by
iss architect Mario Botta.

Yerba Buena Center
The Arts (C C3)
→ 701 Mission St / 3rd St
. 978 2787 / Tue-Sun 11am–
m (8pm 1st Thu of month);
e 1st Tue of month
chnology, sex, racism and
t are themes explored in
e temporary exhibitions
contemporary art in San
ancisco's biggest cultural
mplex (sculpture garden,
lleries).

Cartoon
Museum (C C2)
655 Mission St /3rd St
. 227 8666 /Tue–Sun

11am–5pm; first Tue of the
month: 'pay what you wish'
Housed in what was
previously the Ansel Adams
Center for Photography.
Snoopy, Popeye, Batman
are the permanent hosts in
this museum, which
celebrates the cartoon strip
in all its glorious diversity.
There are more than 11,000
exhibits, some dating from
the 18th century. Kids' area,
CD-Rom gallery and a
wonderful store.

★ Pacific Bell
Ballpark (C E4)
→ King St (between 2nd and
3rd sts). Tel. 972 2000
Classic structure based on
Wrigley Field and Fenway

Park, surrounded by the
dramatic San Francisco
skyline. This $319 million
ballpark, home to the San
Francisco Giants, gives the
best view of the field from
every seat on its 13-acre site.

★ Old United States
Mint (C B3)
→ 5th St / Mission St
With its six Doric columns
and pyramidal exterior
stairway, the former Mint
building is the prime
example of San Francisco's
neoclassical style. Money
was coined here until 1937,
under the protection of thick
granite walls that saved it
from the violent earthquake
of 1906. It is now closed to

the public, as, ironically, it
does not conform to anti-
earthquake regulations.

★ South Park (C D3)
→ Bordered by Bryant,
Brannan, 2nd and 3rd sts
This oval square ringed
with 68 identical redbrick
façades, inspired by
Berkeley Square in London,
has a European atmosphere.
The hub of high society in
the 19th century, an Afro-
American neighborhood in
the 1950s, it now attracts the
thriving new technologies.
The denizens of cyberspace
have taken over its cafés and
hip restaurants, when they
are not picnicking in the
central park area.

HAAS-LILIENTHAL HOUSE

LAFAYETTE PARK

HAYES VALLEY

MC ALLISTER STREET
FULTON STREET
GROVE STREET
ALAMO SQUARE
STREET
HAYES STREET
IVY
LINDEN
STREET
HICKORY
FELL STREET
OAK STREET
PAGE STREET
PAGE STREET
HAIGHT STREET
HAIGHT STREET
WALLER STREET
STREET
HERMANN
DUBOCE PARK
DUBOCE AVENUE
DAVIES MED. CENTER
14TH STREET
DUBOCE
CLINTON
14TH
CHURCH ST.

A   B

★ Cable Car Barn Museum (D D1)

→ *1201 Mason St / Washington St. Tel. 474 1887 www.cablecarmuseum.com April-Sep: daily 10am–6pm Oct-March: daily 10am–5pm;*
A museum, but also the cable cars' engine room. The only system of its kind in the world (1873), inspired by the cabled transport used in mines: motors drag the metal cables buried under the city's streets to pull the beautiful wooden cars. Declared a heritage site in 1964.

★ Nob Hill (D D1)

At 375 ft, this is the highest hill in the city. In the mid-19th century, the new railroad 'nabobs' rushed to build luxurious houses here, attracted by the beautiful views. Destroyed in the 1906 earthquake and fires, the area was rebuilt with Edwardian and Art Deco mansions and hotels.

★ Grace Cathedral (D D2)

→ *1100 California St/ Taylor Tel. 749 6300 Sun-Fri 7am–6pm (7pm Sun); Sat 8am–6pm*
This superb replica (1928–64) of Notre-Dame in Paris, built in reinforced concrete, presides over the top of Nob Hill. It is the city's main Episcopal church and its monumental bronze doorway is particularly imposing: it is a copy of Ghiberti's famous Gates of Paradise, seen in the Duomo's baptistery in Florence, whose panels illustrate scenes from the Old Testament. Organ concerts.

★ Haas-Lilienthal House (D B1)

→ *2007 Franklin St / Washington St. Tel. 441 3004 Wed, Sat noon–3pm; Sun 11am–4pm. Closed bank hols*
Only building in the Queen Anne style open to the public, this 1886 house was built in the typical Eclectic architectural style of the period (molded shingles, barrel vaults in the corner console gables). Extravag interior decoration.

★ Lafayette Park (D B2

There are magnificent view of the bay from the steep steps of the beautiful Lafayette Park, planted wi pines and eucalyptus. The Spreckels Mansion (1913) 2080 Washington St has a impressive stone-carved baroque façade. With a ro of ten Ionic columns, set a against five arched windo it is a neoclassical palace more than a mansion.

★ Japantown (D A3)

→ *Between Fillmore, Post, Laguna sts and Geary Blvd* Shinto temples, pagodas.

D

GRACE CATHEDRAL

NOB HILL

CABLE CAR MUSEUM

Nob Hill / Pacific Heights / Civic Center

Map labels:

GOLDEN GATE AVENUE

TURK STREET

GOLDEN

FILLMORE

STREET

HAYWARD BLDG.

JEFFERSON SQUARE

LAGUNA STREET

ELLIS STREET

EDDY

PIERCE

STEINER

ELLIS

SAINT MARY'S CATHEDRAL

CLEARY CT.

KIMBELL PLGD.

WESTERN ADDITION

STARK WAY

PETER YOR

GEARY BOULEVARD

HAMILTON PLGD.

JAPAN CENTER

POST STREET

SUTTER

JAPANTOWN

STREET

BUSH

WEBSTER

ST.

PINE

STEINER

CALIFORNIA

GOUGH

OCTAVIA

STREET

AUSTIN

STREET

SACRAMENTO

BUCHANAN

PACIFIC PRESBYTERIAN MED. CENTER

CLAY STREET

LAFAYETTE PARK

HAAS-LILIENTHAL HOUSE

RICHARD SPRECKELS MANSION

WASHINGTON STREET

JACKSON STREET

PACIFIC AVENUE

WEBSTER

FILLMORE

FRANKLIN

ST.

GOUGH

STREET

BROADWAY

BUCHANAN STREET

LAGUNA

VALLEJO

GREEN STREET

0 150 300m

FRANKLIN ST. GOUGH STREET VALLEJO STREET

1 2 3 4

A B

Stylish Nob Hill offers panoramic views of the bay and the Financial District skyscrapers. The streets to the south-west bustle with their grocery stores, bars and cafés. Pacific Heights, the area around Lafayette Park is like a twin brother to Nob Hill, with its beautiful examples of Victorian architecture. To the south, the great artery of Geary Street runs alongside Japantown, home to another Asia, perhaps less popular than Chinatown but no less dazzling. To the east, Van Ness Avenue cuts down to the Civic Center, a unique collection of classically designed buildings that make up the administrative and artistic heart of the city.

ZUNI CAFÉ

RESTAURANTS

Isobune Sushi (D A3)
→ *Kinetsu Bldg,*
1737 Post St / Webster St
Tel. 563 1030
Daily 11.30am–10pm
Sushi (more than 70 varieties) and sashimi (sold in 7 or 8 pieces), utterly fresh and superbly presented. Dishes are served on an oval counter, with the chefs working on the other side, or in the small Japanese dining-room. Few Japantown restaurants can match its value for money.
À la carte $15–20.

Swan Oyster Depot (D C2)
→ *1517 Polk St / California St*
Tel. 673 1101
Mon–Sat 8am–5.30pm
Ever since 1912 this oyster seller-cum-restaurant has been regaling the city's residents with super-fresh products: crabs and other shellfish, salmon smoked on the premises etc. Eat at the counter.
À la carte $15–20.

Canto Do Brasil (D C5)
→ *41 Franklin St / Market St*
Tel. 626 8727
Mon–Fri 11am–3pm, 5–9pm
(10pm Fri); Sat 11am–10pm;
Sun 5–9pm
Shellfish sautéed with garlic in pineapple and coconut sauce, seafood paella, *feijoada* (black bean stew) and other Brazilian delicacies in this charming yellow and pale blue restaurant. À la carte $18–25.

Suppenküche (D B5)
→ *601 Hayes St / Laguna St*
Tel. 252 9289 / Mon–Sat
5–10pm; Sun 10am– 2.30pm,
5–10pm; closed bank hols.
Further proof of San Francisco's culinary eclecticism, this German restaurant has recreated a Bavarian setting (large rustic wooden tables) in the heart of Hayes Valley. The highlights are the *Wiener Schnitzel* (pork and roast potatoes), lentil soup and, of course, *sauerkraut.*
À la carte $20–25.

Zuni Café (D C5)
→ *1658 Market St / Franklin St*
Tel. 552 2522
Mon–Sat 11.30am–midnight;
Sun 11am–midnight; closed
bank hols.
Italian-Californian cooking using top-quality produce: tender chicken, roasted according to a traditional recipe, a range of small pizzas, plates of oysters on a bed of ice. Plus an unrestricted view of the ceaseless bustle of Market Street. Superb selection of wines from France, Italy, Spain and California.

ACE PIGALLE

PSYCHIC EYE

WHOLE FOODS

À la carte $30.

Jardinière (D C4)
→ 300 Grove St / Franklin St
Tel. 861 5555
Daily 5–10.30pm
An Art Deco setting for French cooking at its most refined (tuna *tartare*, risotto with chanterelles, duck confit with figs and pistachios). Mouthwatering desserts: caramelized pear with gingerbread, chocolate fondant cake, sorbets.
À la carte $75.

ICE CREAM PARLOR

Perry's Joint (D A3)
→ 1661 Fillmore St / Sutter St
Tel. 931 5260 Mon-Sat
8am–9pm; Sun noon–6pm
Great stop-off for peckish walkers, just a few yards away from the Japan Center. Multicolored candies, delicious ice creams (green tea, banana, tiramisu, butter pecan, mango flavors), coffees and snacks, all to a soundtrack of jazz.

BARS, CONCERT VENUES, OPERA

Place Pigalle (D B5)
→ 520 Hayes St / Octavia St
Tel. 552 2671
Sun-Wed 4pm–midnight
(2am Thu-Sat)

Enormous sofas and cozy armchairs, a pool table and exhibition area at the back: this bar cultivates a hip, artistic atmosphere that is very popular among the young people of Hayes Valley. Beer and Californian red wines.

Edinburgh Castle (D C3)
→ 950 Geary St / Larkin St
Tel. 885 4074
Daily 5pm–2am
Focal point of the British community in San Francisco, this pub serves generous portions of fish and chips plus 20 varieties of English beers. Hotly disputed games of darts and free concerts four nights a week (reggae, jazz, rock, punk).

Red Devil Lounge (D C1)
→ 1695 Polk St / Clay St
Tel. 921 1695
Mon-Sat 7pm–2am
An intimate setting for concerts by budding rock stars and sessions by local DJs.

The Great American Music Hall (D C3)
→ 859 O'Farrell St / Larkin St. Tel. 885 0750
Times depend on program
The city's oldest music hall, built in 1907. All the magic of a unique venue: wonderful rococo décor (ornate circles, pillars, huge mirrors) that oozes

history (Duke Ellington and Sarah Vaughan performed here). High-quality program of jazz and rock. Varying prices.

War Memorial Opera House (D C4)
→ 301 Van Ness / Grove St.
Tel. 861 4008
www.sfopera.com
Box office at 199 Grove St
(tel. 864 4330)
Times depend on program
This cultural treasure has been attracting the world's greatest singers and dancers ever since 1923. The city raised almost $90 million to seismically retrofit the building after it was seriously damaged in the 1989 earthquake. Performances by the San Francisco Opera and the San Francisco Ballet.

SHOPPING

Kinokuniya Bookstore (D A3)
→ 1581 Webster St / Post St
(in the Japan Center)
Tel. 567 7625
Daily 10.30am–8pm
Japantown's Kinokuniya Bookstore may be the biggest collection of books on Japanese culture you've ever seen under one roof. Topics range from history to cooking. Volumes are available in

English as well as Japanese.

Gimme Shoes (D C4)
→ 416 Hayes St / Gough St
Tel. 864 0691 / Mon-Sat
11am–7pm; Sun noon–6pm
European designers (Prada, Miumiu, Robert Clergerie) for men's and women's shoes in original and daring forms.

Psychic Eye Book Shop (D C5)
→ 301 Fell St / Gough St
Tel. 863 9997 / Mon-Sat
10am–10pm; Sun 11am–7pm
Ali Baba's magic cavern! Candles, oils, African gris-gris, kits for Indian ceremonies: everything an apprentice magician could possibly require. Tarot readings in the back.

Ross (D C2)
→ 1645 Van Ness Ave / California St. Tel. 775 0192
Mon-Sat 9.30am–9pm; Sun 11am–7pm
Discount prices for the top names in fashion (Calvin Klein, DKNY, Levi's, Esprit, Reebok), for the whole family.

Whole Foods (D B2)
→ 1765 California St / Franklin St. Tel. 674 0500
Daily 8am–10pm
The supermarket for Downtown gourmets with organic produce, fruit and vegetables, condiments, wines, cheeses, cakes and natural cosmetics.

↑ Map C

CITY HALL

ST MARY'S CATHEDRAL

↑ Map B

JAPANTOWN

VETERANS
BUILDING

CITY
CENTER

SAN FRANCISCO

ASIAN ART
MUSEUM

United
Nations
Plaza

CIVIC
CENTER

CALLISTER

GOLDEN GATE AVENUE

TURK

STREET

TENDERLOIN

VAN NESS

ELLIS

O'FARRELL

GEARY

POST

SUTTER

BUSH

ST. FRANCIS
MEM. HOSP.

PINE

CALIFORNIA

SACRAMENTO

GRACE
CATHEDRAL

NOB HILL

CABLE CAR
BARN MUSEUM

CLAY

WASHINGTON

JACKSON

PACIFIC
AVENUE

BROADWAY

VALLEJO

MASON

TAYLOR

JONES

LEAVENWORTH

HYDE

POLK

LARKIN

STREET

STEVENSON

7TH STREET

STREET

HYDE ST.

STREET

JONES STREET

POLK

STREET

HYDE ST.

LARKIN STREET

LEAVENWORTH

TAYLOR ST.

POLK STREET

LARKIN

LEAVENWORTH

HYDE ST.

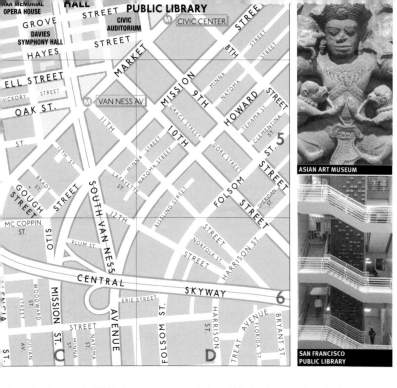

ASIAN ART MUSEUM

SAN FRANCISCO PUBLIC LIBRARY

rdens and tea houses rub oulders with Victorian uses in the six blocks of is 12,000-strong Japanese clave. The ighborhood's social life volves around the untless shops and sushi rs of the Japan Center, ilt around the Peace onument, a replica of a ditional pagoda.

St Mary's thedral (D B3)
→ 1111 Gough St / Geary vd Tel. 567 2020 ily 6.45am–5.30pm e Catholic cathedral 971) offers the bizarre cture of a boat with white ils on the top of Cathedral Hill. Modern structure (four supporting vaults in travertine, reinforced concrete cupola) and airy interior (aluminium canopy, stained-glass windows in the form of a cross above the nave).

★ City Hall (D C4)
→ 1 Dr Carlton B. Goodlett Place. Tel. 554 4000
Mon-Fri 8am–8pm;
Sat-Sun noon–4pm
The most imposing and elaborate monument in San Francisco (1915), and the masterpiece of its architects Bakewell and Brown. Looking out on a spacious esplanade, the City Hall seems to follow a textbook design, with Doric columns and rows of colonnades. Inside, a pink marble staircase leads to a rotunda topped with a baroque cupola inspired by St Peter's in Rome and, in a piece of one-upmanship, higher than the Capitol in Washington.

★ San Francisco Public Library (D D4)
→ 100 Larkin St / Grove St Tel. 557 4400
Mon & Sat 10am–6pm;
Tue-Thu 9am–8pm;
Fri noon–6pm (5pm Sun);
closed bank hols
A successful mix of modern and traditional, the new library (1996) beautifully echoes the facing City Hall (the architect used the same white stone). There is more modernism inside, with a breathtaking atrium illuminated by natural light.

★ Asian Art Museum (D D4)
→ SF Main Library, Fulton St / Larkin St. Tel. 581 3500
Tue-Sun 10am–5pm (9pm Thu); free 1st tue of month
The city's former library, damaged by the 1989 earthquake, was renovated to house the Asian Art Museum: a priceless collection of 12,000 pieces (jade, bronzes, pottery, sculptures, etc.) illustrating 6,000 years of Asian art.

JAPANESE TEA GARDEN

TWIN PEAKS

★ **Alamo Square (E** E1)
Half the city's postcards seem to feature this leafy 19th-century square, lined with splendid Victorian houses: it offers a striking contrast with the Downtown skyscrapers, which it dominates by some 230 ft. On Steiner Street can be found the city's most beautiful row of six 'painted ladies': elegant wooden houses with gables and painted façades. Built in 1895, they originally sold for under $6,000 each!

★ **Haight Street (E** D2)
This spacious backwater between the Golden Gate and Buena Vista parks

offers a retreat from the bustle of the city's center. In the 1960s, its multicultural atmosphere and cheap rents attracted young people in search of freedom, culminating in the hippie movement. The crossroads of Haight and Ashbury has retained a unique bohemian feel, with its host of cafés and 'head shops.'

★ **Golden Gate Park (E** B-C2)
→ *Main entrance: John F. Kennedy Drive, near Stanyan St. Regular, free, walking guided tours.*
Spread over more than 1,000 acres, this is the biggest landscaped urban

park in the country. In 1871, when work on the park began, this huge area stretching from Stanyan Boulevard to Ocean Beach was nothing more than sandy scrub land, and the landscape gardeners needed all their ingenuity to exploit this desolate, supposedly barren terrain. Soil enrichment techniques, the wealth of freshly planted trees and the 1894 International Exposition finally sealed the park's international reputation. Today, this breathing space boasts many sports facilities, three museums, lakes, esplanades, play

areas for all kinds of sport and paths for cycling, walking and horseback riding.

★ **California Academy of Sciences (E** A2)
→ *55 Concourse Drive, Gold Gate Park. Tel. 750 7145 www.calacademy.org Sep-May: daily 10am–5pm June-Aug: daily 9am–6pm; free 1st Wed of the month 10am–8.45pm*
The oldest scientific institution in the West (18 includes the Steinhart Aquarium (more than 6,0 aquatic species), the Morrison Planetarium and a huge natural history museum (ecosystems,

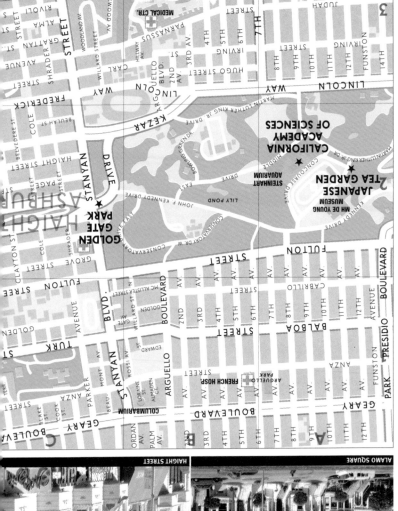

Alamo Square, on the edge of Pacific Heights, offers a last look Downtown. Two blocks to the south lies Haight Street, the birthplace of the hippie movement, which has turned somewhat middle-class: European style-cafés, hip stores and Bohemian posers lead the way to the Golden Gate Park, an enormous green area going down to the sea. To the southeast, sheltered from the fogs of the bay, sunny Castro, the gay neighborhood, borders on Market Street. Beyond that lies the Mission, the oldest part of the city: taco joints, brightly colored murals and an atmoshere of *mucha movida* in this Latin American enclave.

TI COUZ   CHA CHA CHA

RESTAURANTS

Pancho Villa Taqueria
(**E** F3, off map)
→ 3071 16th St at Valencia St
Tel. 864 8840
Daily 10am–midnight
Don't be fooled by the typical Mission burrito-joint look of this place. It is generally regarded as one of the best *taquerias* in the city. The menu is more extensive than most in its category and the food is really good. The chicken filling can be prepared in different ways; beef tongue and vegetarian options are available; the tortillas come in different colors, which is always a hit with the children. À la carte $4–7.

Ti Couz (**E** F3)
→ 3108 16th St / Valencia St
Tel. 252 7373
Mon-Wed 11am–11pm (midnight Thu-Fri); Sat 10am–midnight (11pm Sun); closed Thanksgiving & Dec 24
Delicious pancakes, savory (mushrooms, egg tomato, cheese) or sweet (chocolate, cream, jam) in the authentic all-wood décor of a French *crêperie*. Dry cider (bowl or pitcher). À la carte $12–20.

Limón (**E** F3, off map)
→ 3316 17th St, between Mission and Valencia
Tel. 252 0918 / Tue-Thu
11.30am–9.30pm (10.30pm Fri); Sat-Sun 11.30am–9pm
Owner and executive chef Martin Castillo has created an instant favorite with the mouthwatering authentic and fusion Peruvian cuisine served in two brightly colored rooms. The lively crowd comes for the ceviche and steak, pork chops and seafood as well as the fruit ice cream flown in from Peru. À la carte $8–17.

Cha Cha Cha (**E** C2)
→ 1801 Haight St / Shrader St
Tel. 386 5758 /
Daily 11.30am–4pm, 5–11pm (11.30pm Fri-Sat)
In this beautiful blue building, a Hispano-Caribbean restaurant full of plants, Madonnas and Inca statuettes you can find a variety of tapas (fried squid, spiced shrimps, grilled chicken), sandwiches (spiced chicken, cream cheese, salmon with Cajun sauce) and traditional Caribbean dishes (*arroz con pollo*: chicken marinated in chili with rice and black beans). À la carte $20–25.

Delfina (**E** F3)
→ 3621 18th St / Dolores St
Tel. 552 4055 / Daily 5.30–10pm (10.30pm Fri-Sat)
Daily changing menu of mouthwatering Italian and Californian cuisine dishes (salt cod brandade, fresh

STRO THEATER

PLANET WEAVERS

VILLAINS

grilled calamari, local fish, pasta, buttermilk pannacotta) have made this a favorite spot. Book ahead, and arrive early to be able to find a parking space. À la carte $15–30.

CAFÉS

Dolores Café (E F3)
→ 501 Dolores St / 18th St
Tel. 621 2936
Daily 7am–8pm
This very popular European-style café offers magnificent views over the hills of Dolores Park. Sandwiches, salads, teas and coffees. Pleasant summer terrace.

Cafe Macondo (E F3)
→ 3159 16th St / Guerrero St. Tel. 431 7516
Mon–Fri 10am–10pm; Sat 11am–10pm
The coziest of all the Mission's cafés. Old armchairs, comfortable sofas, pink and violet walls and jazz in the background. Small bookshelves with all kinds of books, for reading on the premises. Coffee and homemade cakes.

BARS, NIGHTCLUBS MOVIE THEATERS

Elbo Room (E F3)
→ 17th St / Valencia St

Tel. 552 7788
Daily 5pm–2am; closed Christmas & Jan 1
Dive into the boisterous world of Latin nightlife in the Mission's most popular nightclub. The bar is on the ground floor, the 1st floor is where you can dance to live salsa, samba or merengue.

Mad Dog in the Fog (E F2)
→ 530 Haight St / Fillmore St
Tel. 626 7279
Mon–Fri 11.30am–2am; Sat–Sun 10am–2am
A highly successful compromise between an English pub, a sports bar and a concert hall, with local punk, rock and reggae bands playing live. No cover charge (except for watching soccer matches).

The Café (E E3)
→ 2367 Market St / Castro St
Tel. 861 3846
Mon–Fri 2pm–2am; Sat–Sun 12.30pm–2am
One of Castro's most popular gay bars, completely in the thrall of electronic music. Very spacious premises (bar, two dance floors, balcony, mezzanine). Free entry.

Nickie's BBQ (E F2)
→ 460 Haight St / Fillmore St / Tel. 621 6508
Daily 9pm–2am

Funk, reggae, hiphop, soul, jungle, disco, world music... this trend-setting club on Lower Haight explores a different musical theme every night.

Castro Theater (E E3)
→ 429 Castro St / Market St
Tel. 621 6120
Independent movies and retrospectives of major international directors in the city's most prestigious cinema. Beautiful baroque-style auditorium with a giant screen and a genuine Wurlitzer organ. Tickets $8.

SHOPPING

Amoeba Music (E C2)
→ 1855 Haight St / Stanyan
Tel. 831 1200
Mon–Sat 10.30am–10pm; Sun 11am–9pm
The best record store in town, housed in an old bowling rink. Impressive choice of CDs, vinyl records and DVDs, both new and secondhand, in every conceivable musical style (with a particularly well-stocked Indian music section).

Bi-Rite Market (E F3)
→ 3639 18th St / Dolores St
Tel. 241 9773
Mon–Fri 9am–9pm (8pm Sat–Sun)
A grocery store that goes

back more than 50 years: freshly-made bread, cheese (over 100 varieties), sausages, salmon smoked on the premises and salads to take out. Ideal for stocking up for a picnic in Dolores Park.

Global Exchange Fair Trade Craft Center (E E4)
→ 4018 24th St (between Noe and Castro sts)
Tel. 648 8068
Daily 11am–7pm
www.globalexchange.org/store
This huge store supports and promotes fair trade, selling unique craft goods from all over the world, from Nepalese jewelry to hand-knitted Guatemalan pullovers.

Planet Weavers Treasure Store (E D2)
→ 1573 Haight St / Ashbury St / Tel. 864 4415
Daily 10am–8pm
Wonderful store packed with ideas for presents: candles, cosmetics, Japanese-inspired mobiles, jewelry, new age music...

Villains (E C2)
→ 1653 & 1672 Haight St / Cole St. Tel. 626 5939
Daily 11am–7pm
Street fashion and shoes for both sexes spread over three shops: trousers in light but warm material, vests, T-shirts, etc.

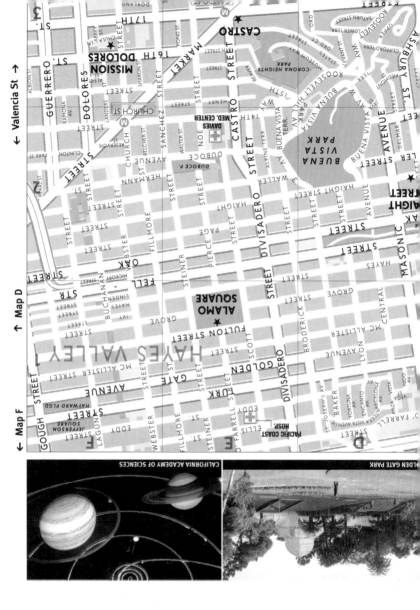

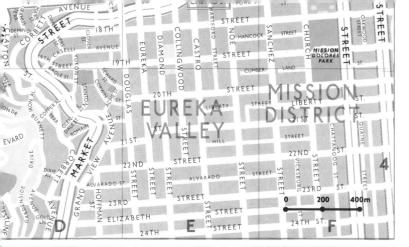

CASTRO

MISSION DOLORES

ace and planets section, lleries on evolution, etc.).

Japanese a Garden (E A2)

*Golden Gate Park (on nnedy Drive) Tel. 668 0909
en daily:
ril-Aug: 9am– 6.30pm
p-March: 8.30am–5.30pm
aroom 10am–5.15pm*

u will find a maze of nding paths, pools with ooden bridges, a pagoda, ntems, a Buddha, a Zen rden and bonsai in this quisite 5-acre Japanese rden, created for the 1894 ternational Exhibition. agical when the cherry es are blossoming. the tea house at the foot

of the pagoda, kimono-clad waiters serve drinks, fortune cookies and rice cakes.

★ Castro (E E3)

→ *Between 18th and Market, Douglas, and Dolores sts*

This heart of San Francisco's gay community is built on the land of an old Mexican ranch. In the early 1960s the gay population began to buy up the Victorian houses and lovingly restored them. These days the hilly streets of this lively neighborhood are flanked by hip bars and shopfronts, either elegant or outrageous. Rainbow-colored flags, the symbol of homosexual identity, flutter all down Market Street and

hang from many windows in the area, as a reminder of the hard struggles of gay activism.

★ Mission Dolores (E F3)

→ *320 Dolores St / 16th St
Tel. 621 8203
Daily 9am– 4.30pm (4pm Nov-March)*

This is the doyen of the city's buildings, a testimony to San Francisco's Latin heritage. Founded in 1776, this 6th Catholic mission in Upper California has, since 1982, boasted a Spanish colonial-style chapel and an austere adobe façade with buttresses and pillars. Lavish interior decoration: sequoia beams, a ceiling

adorned with Ohlone motifs and an eye-catching baroque altarpiece. Museum and historic cemetery.

★ Twin Peaks (E D4)

→ *Twin Peaks Blvd*

These two hills soar 903 and 910 feet above the city. According to an Ohlone Indian legend, the two twin daughters of a chief were frozen there for eternity by the Great Spirit. The hills are largely untouched: only one boulevard winds up to the belvedere of Christmas Tree Point, where there are breathtaking views of the north and east of San Francisco.

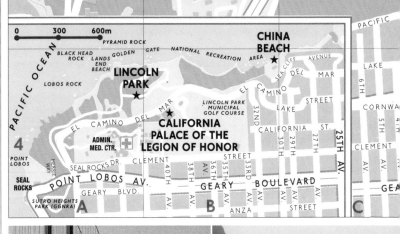

GOLDEN GATE BRIDGE

CHINA BEACH

★ The Presidio (F D3)
→ *Lombard St / Lyon St (main entrance) Visitor Center at 50 Moraga Ave Tel. 561 4323*
More than 150 years of Californian military architecture unfold on this 1,480-acre site, planted with pine and redwood trees; with miles of hiking and biking and some of the most spectacular vistas in the world, this is an amazing site for nature lovers.

★ Fort Point (F B1)
→ *At the end of Marine Drive Tel. 556 1693 / Wed-Sun 10am–5pm; closed bank hols*
Strategically located at the entrance to San Francisco Bay, this redbrick and granite fort still has an imposing presence. It was built in 1861 on the site of an old Spanish fortification, to protect the city from sea attack. This jewel of military architecture points its 126 cannons at the Golden Gate channel. The raised platform, lashed by winds from the bay, offers dizzying views of the bridge and the rocky shoreline.

★ Palace of Fine Arts (F E2)
→ *Baker St / Beach St www.exploratorium.edu/palace*
A rotunda with allegorical bas-reliefs, a maze of Corinthian columns on the shores of a peaceful pond... Nestling in the fog of The Presidio, this most romantic of all the city's sights has the feel of ancient ruins. The anachronisms are deliberate: to create this masterpiece for the 1915 International Exhibition, its architect Bernard Maybeck sought inspiration in Arnold Böcklin's painting *The Island of the Dead* and the engravings of Piranesi (1720–78). Originally built in plaster, it was recast in concrete, in 1967, thanks to private donations.

★ Exploratorium Science Museum (F E2)
→ *Palace of Fine Arts, 3601 Lyon St. Tel. 561 0360 www.exploratorium.edu Tue-Sun 10am–5pm; free 1 Wed of month*
This is a museum of science and perception, a pioneer in interactive exhibitions (1969). The secrets of electrical, climatic and sensory phenomena revealed in hundreds of experiments. Don't miss Tactile Dome: a sensory journey in total darkness (reservations advised).

★ Golden Gate Bridge (F B1)
→ *Golden Gate Freeway, Presidio Park. Tel. 921 5858 www.goldengatebridge.or Pedestrian sidewalk: daily*

F

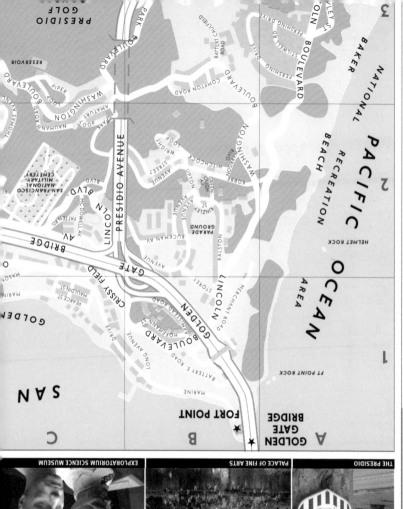

THE PRESIDIO

PALACE OF FINE ARTS

EXPLORATORIUM SCIENCE MUSEUM

PRESIDIO GOLF

RESERVOIR

PIPER

NAUMANN ROAD BOULEVARD

THOMAS AVENUE

WASHINGTON BOULEVARD

PARK BOULEVARD

PARK LOOP

AMATURY LOOP

BATTERY CAULFIELD ROAD

COMPTON ROAD

STILWELL RD

PERSHING DRIVE

PERSHING DRIVE

BAKER

NATIONAL

PACIFIC

RECREATION BEACH

OCEAN

AREA

HELMET ROCK

SAN FRANCISCO NATIONAL MILITARY CEMETERY

PRESIDIO AVENUE

LINCOLN BLVD

MCDOWELL AV

PATTERSON

WRIGHT LOOP

AVENUE

HITCHCOCK LOOP

KOBBE AVENUE

GREENOUGH ST

UPTON STREET

VINZEL AVENUE

WASHINGTON BLVD

RALSTON

PARADE GROUND

RUCKMAN AV

AVENUE

STOREY

MERCHANT ROAD

LINCOLN

BOULEVARD

FT POINT ROCK

BRIDGE

GATE

GOLDEN

LINCOLN

MASON

MARIN

PEARCE ST

MAULDIN ST

CRISSY FIELD

DRIVE

LONG AVENUE

HOFFMANN ST

HALLECK ROAD

BATTERY E ROAD

MARINE

GOLDEN

SAN

FORT POINT

GOLDEN GATE BRIDGE

Precipitous cliffs, gusts of sea wind: a wild and rugged San Francisco can be found at the northwestern tip of the peninsula. To the north, the vast expanses of The Presidio, once used for military purposes, extend to the Golden Gate Bridge: Fort Point practically touches the great metal giant. To the west, Lincoln Park nestles on top of steep cliffs that border the raging Pacific Ocean. Between these two green areas, Richmond, the city's biggest neighborhood is almost too neat, despite the mix of cafés, grocery stores and restaurants stretching down Clement Street.

ELLA'S

RESTAURANTS

King of Thai Noodle House (F C4)
→ 639 Clement St / 7th Ave
Tel. 752 5198
Daily 11am–1.30am
This restaurant is famous for its good value and its décor. Specialties are noodle soup (with seafood, shrimps, beef or chicken) and rice dishes. À la carte $7–10.

Ella's (F C4)
→ 500 Presidio Ave / California St. Tel. 441 5669
Mon–Fri 7–11am, 11.30am–4pm, 5–9pm; Brunch: Sat-Sun 8.30am–2m
Good, simple food is served here during the week but it is the week-end brunch – the best in town – that has made Ella's a Pacific Heights institution. It is worth queing for such classics as cold meats, Italian cheese, a variety of omelets, muffins, housemade sticky buns, buttermilk pancakes, fruit crumbles and bagels. Children should like this place. Brunch $8.

Café Presidio (F C-D3)
→ 300 Finley Road at the Arguello Gates
Tel. 561 4661 Mon-Fri 11.30am–3pm; Sat 11am–3pm; Sun 10am–3pm
You don't need to exhaust yourself with a day of golf to enjoy the Café Presidio, located in the Presidio Golf Course's clubhouse. The dining room is lovely, boasting a stone fireplace and picture windows, and the food is light and flavorful. Before Sunday brunch, live jazz is featured from 10am–2pm.
À la carte $7–12.

Minh's Garden (F D4)
→ 208 Clement St / 3rd Ave
Tel. 751 8211
Mon–Thu 11am–10pm (10.30pm Fri–Sat);
Sun 6–10pm
Assorted soups, fried fish, stir-fried shrimps (with broccoli, with coconut milk and curry or with lemon grass) and other classics of Vietnamese cuisine, in this beautiful restaurant, highly prized by gourmets.
À la carte $10.

Clementine (F D4)
→ 126 Clement St / 2nd Ave
Tel. 387 0408
Sun–Thu 5.30pm–10pm (10.30pm Fri–Sat)
The first impression when you step inside Clementine is of casual elegance and romanticism (small building covered with Virginia creeper, a street-corner bistro with wall seats); then comes the treat of a refined, if classic,

Y BOAT DESSERT CAFE

KAMEI RESTAURANT SUPPLY

IMAGINARIUM

French cuisine (salmon in sorrel sauce, roasted quails with four spices and honey, chicken *grand-mère*). Affordable and extensive wine list. À la carte $35.

CAFÉ, TEAROOM

Java Source Coffee House (F C4)
➔ 343 Clement St / 4th Ave
Tel. 387 8025 / Daily 7am–midnight (1am Fri-Sat)
The main attraction of this huge cream and brown café is its big covered terrace on Clement St. You can settle down at a table with a muffin and a cappuccino, and read for hours. Chess classes.

Toy Boat Dessert Cafe (F C4)
➔ 401 Clement St / 5th Ave
Tel. 751 7505
Mon–Thu 7.30am–11pm (midnight Fri);
Sun 8.30am–11pm
A cross between a tea room and a toy store, this café-cum-ice cream parlor cultivates a colorful childlike atmosphere, with soft toys and figures of the top comic-strip heroes rubbing shoulders with multicolored candies on the shelves. Coffee, hot chocolate, cakes and ice creams.

PUBS, MUSIC BAR

Bitter End (F C4)
➔ 441 Clement St / 5th Ave
Tel. 221 9538
Mon–Fri 3pm–2am;
Sat–Sun 10am–2am
A beautiful shopfront in the form of a green bottle leads into a bar where regular customers thrive on the warm, intimate atmosphere: soft lighting, pub-style wooden paneling, a big old counter at the back, a pool table and a dartboard. Hot dishes (burgers, shepherd's pies); copious brunch at weekends.

Liverpool Lil's (F E2)
➔ 2942 Lyon St / Lombard
Tel. 921 6664
Mon–Fri 11am–2am;
Sat-Sun 10am–2am
This typical English pub is an ideal spot for unwinding over a pint with friends. Try to come during the happy hour (4–6pm): the drinks are the same price, but there are free snacks (ravioli, roast chicken...).

The Plough and Stars (F D4)
➔ 116 Clement St / 2nd Ave
Tel. 751 1122
Daily 2pm–2am
Good neighborhood bar playing Irish folk music

(live Tue-Fri). Monday evenings are given over to marathon sessions of a trivia game. The small but excellent selection of English and Irish beers, both draft and bottled, along with the fiddles, attract San Francisco's Irish community. Cover charge at the weekend.

SHOPPING

Kamei Restaurant Supply (F C4)
➔ 507 Clement St / 6th Ave
Tel. 666 3699
Daily 9am–7pm
A huge range of chromium-plated kitchen utensils and wonderful Chinese and Japanese tableware (tea services, bowls, plates, chopsticks) line the walls like goods in a hardware store. The prices are unbeatable.

Vinh Khang Herbs & Ginsengs (F C4)
➔ 512 Clement St (between 6th and 7th aves)
Tel. 752 8336
Wed–Mon 9.30am–7pm
An authentic traditional Chinese herbalist's shop, with a wide range of roots with medicinal properties. All the minor ills of everyday life (heartburn, migraines, insomnia) can be dispelled by the right

mix of therapeutic herbs.

Green Apple Books and Music (F C4)
➔ 506 Clement St / 6th Ave
Tel. 387 2272
Sun-Thu 10am–10.30pm (11.30pm Fri-Sat)
www.greenapplebooks.com
Laser discs, vinyl records (rock and classical), DVDs, detective stories... new or second-hand.

California Wine Merchant (F F2)
➔ 3237 Pierce St / Chestnut St
Tel. 567 0646
Mon-Sat 11am–7pm;
Sun noon–5pm
Fancy a good Merlot or a Pinoit Noir? This store specializing in American wines offers an excellent selection of vintages from both California and the northern Pacific coastal region. Helpful, knowledgeable staff and an overseas shipping service.

Imaginarium (F D4)
➔ Laurel Shopping Center, 3535 California St / Spruce St
Tel. 387 9885
Mon-Sat 9.30am–7pm;
Sun 10am–5pm
You can find highly unusual, beautiful toys for children here. Definitely not for fans of Barbie dolls.

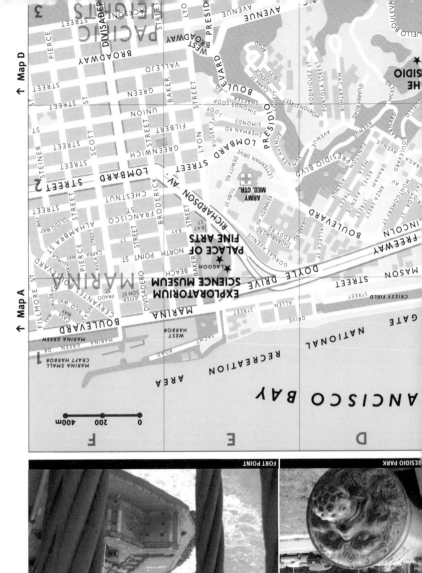

PACIFIC HEIGHTS

3

JACKSON STREET

PIERCE STREET

DIVISADERO STREET

BROADWAY

AVENUE

LYO

WEST BROADWAY

PRESID

VALLEJO

GREEN STREET

BAKER STREET

UNION

STEINER STREET

SCOTT STREET

FILBERT STREET

GREENWICH STREET

PRESIDIO BOULEVARD

BOULEVARD

ST.

ST.

ST.

LYON STREET

RUGER'S RD

SHAFTER

JELLY

LETTERMAN AVENUE

CLEMENT

MORTON STREET

RODRIGUEZ ST

MAC ARTHUR

QUARRY ROAD

PORTOLA STREET

SIMONDS LOOP

SIMONDS

SHERMAN RD

AVENUE

FUNSTON AVENUE

AVENUE

STREET 2

LOMBARD

CHESTNUT STREET

CHESTNUT ST.

ALHAMBRA ST

STREET

TOLEDO WAY

PIERCE WAY

CAPRA WAY

AVILA ST

FRANCISCO STREET

BRODERICK AV.

RICHARDSON AV.

BAY ST

BAY STREET

LETTERMAN DRIVE

DEWITT RD

KEITH AVENUE

EDD ST

THORNBURG ST

★ ARMY MED. CTR.

TORNEY AVENUE

PRESIDIO BLVD

GORGAS AVENUE

GRAHAM STREET

ANZA STREET

RILEY AVENUE

KEYES AVENUE

GRAHAM STREET

GIRARD ROAD

HALLECK STREET

MONTGOMERY ST

MESA STREET

RICHARDSON

BAKER STREET

NORTH POINT ST.

PALACE OF FINE ARTS

★ LAGOON

★ EXPLORATORIUM

SCIENCE MUSEUM

BEACH

MARINA BOULEVARD

JEFFERSON ST

PICO WAY

RICO WAY

CASA WAY

CERVANTES BLVD

PRADO ST

DIVISADERO

MARINA

DOYLE DRIVE

DRIVE

ALLEN STREET

LINCOLN BOULEVARD

MASON STREET

HALLECK STREET

FREEWAY

LINCOLN

CHRISSY FIELD STREET

MASON

STREET

FILLMORE ST

MARINA GREEN DR

GREEN

WEST HARBOR

ROAD

YACHT

RECREATION

AREA

GATE

NATIONAL

DRIVE

CRISSY FIELD STREET

BAGA AVENUE

PALMAYOR BOULEVARD

MONTGOMERY ST

RIDGE RD

MARINA SMALL CRAFT HARBOR

1

ANCISCO BAY

THE PRESIDIO ★

JELLO BOULEVARD

400m

200

0

F

E

D

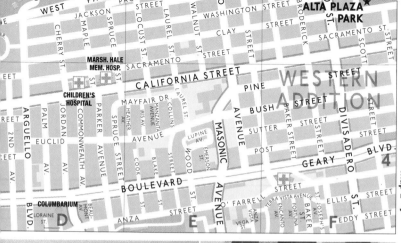

NCOLN PARK

CALIFORNIA PALACE OF THE LEGION OF HONOR

m–9pm (6am–6pm winter) he orange outline of this t Deco bridge, designed y Joseph Strauss, straddles e point where the rbulent waters of the acific meet those of the ay. Four years (1933–37),),000 miles of steel wire in e cables and a budget of 35 million were required to ect this 1.7-mile link etween the San Francisco eninsula and Marin ounty. This is one of the ngest suspension bridge the world, and one of he rongest. A long pedestrian dewalk leads from San ancisco down the eastern de of the bridge, 220 feet

above the water: goosepimples and stunning views guaranteed.

★ China Beach (F B4)
→ Sea Cliff Ave
In the 19th century, this peaceful sandy cove, sheltered from the gusty winds of the bay, housed a camp for Chinese fishermen. The beach is now given over to sunbathing and swimming.

★ Lincoln Park (F A4)
In the 1920s San Francisco families flocked to this area to enjoy the fairground at the edge of the sea. Now returned to its wild state, this strip of rugged land boasts plunging cliffs and

sleepy creeks bordered by paths with panoramic views. The Cliff House, a former inn overlooking the ocean, and now a restaurant, is an ideal vantage point for the brown pelicans and sea lions sheltered by Seal Rocks.

★ California Palace of the Legion of Honor (F B4)
→ 100 34th Ave Lincoln Park
Tel. 863 3330
www.thinker.org / Tue–Sun 9.30am–5pm; free Tue
An elegant neoclassical replica (1924) of the Palais de la Légion d'Honneur in Paris, renovated and enlarged in 1995. The art collection, assembled by

Alma Spreckels, the wife of the sugar magnate, includes Egyptian antiquities, 17th- and 18th-century British, Dutch and Flemish painting sculptures by Rodin, and 70,000 drawings and prints.

★ Alta Plaza Park (F F3)
→ Scott St (betweeen Jackson and Clay sts)
This park affords wonderful views over Twin Peaks and Downtown, and is an ideal starting point for an archi- tectural tour of Victorian San Francisco. Don't miss Boum Mansion (2250 Webster St), and Whittier Mansions (2090 Jackson St), two jewels in one of the most select parts of town.

FROM THE AIRPORTS TO SAN FRANCISCO

By taxi
→ Price $40 (SFO), $60 (OA)
Give 15% of the cost of the journey as a tip.
By shuttle
Links provided by several private shuttle services. Departures every 20 mins, price $15.
Bay Shuttle
→ Tel. 564 3400
Super Shuttle (SFO)
→ Tel. 558 8500
By bus
The lines KX ($3.50/ 35 mins) and 292 ($2.50/ 55 mins) link SFO with Transbay Terminal (1st St/ Mission St).

BART TRAIN

$90–$150

Hotel Milano (C B3)
→ 55 5ᵗʰ St (between Market and Mission sts)
Tel. 543 8555
This renovated eight-storey 1920s hotel, near the Moscone Convention Center, has a screening room and caters to the movie crowd. With décor inspired by Giorgio Armani's Milan villa, the 108 modern rooms have many electronic amenities; Padovani's restaurant offers 24-hour room service. $99–$279.

Golden Gate Hotel (B B6)
→ 775 Bush St /Powell St
Tel. 392 3702
All the charm of a British bed-and-breakfast, and the city's oldest elevator, in this beautiful Victorian building (1913) in Nob Hill. Cozy rooms (carpet, Liberty fabrics), with (from $115) or without (from $85) bathroom – including tea. No smoking.

Beresford Arms (D D2)
→ 701 Post St / Jones St
Tel. 673 2600
Elegance and comfort are the touchstones in this huge hotel between Chinatown and Union Square. The imposing lobby (chandeliers and molding) leads to 195 spacious rooms (some with kitchen). From $139; warm welcome and tea offered in the afternoon.

Radisson Miyako Hotel (D A3)
→ 1625 Post St / Fillmore St
Tel. 922 3200
A winning mix of modern comfort and Oriental lifestyle in the heart of Japantown. The 200 spacious rooms (cable TV, large bathrooms, Japanese furniture, minibar, hairdryer) overlook exquisite Zen gardens. Steam baths and tatamis in the suites. From $129; $232 with diner for two and Japanese bath.

Petite Auberge (B A6)
→ 863 Bush St / Mason St
Tel. 928 6000
A little piece of England! The Petite Auberge is modeled on an English country cottage: floral wallpaper, rustic furniture in the 25 rooms, fireplaces... and tea and cakes at 4pm (incl.). $145; $245 for a suite on ground floor with private entrance and jacuzzi.

$150–$180

King George Hotel (C B2)
→ 334 Mason St /O'Farell St
Tel. 781 5050
This beautiful bow-windowed green building (1912) is a classic example of the city's stylish, early 20th-century architecture. Its 143 rooms marry elegance with comfort. Internet access and video games. From $150.

Dockside Boat & Bed (B B2)
→ Pier 39, Dock C
www.boatandbed.com

CARS

San Francisco is best appreciated on foot, but the public transport network is very efficient. Renting a car is also an option.
Speed limit
In the city
25 miles/hr
Highways and freeways
55-65 miles/hr
Parking
On sloping streets, parking is often only permitted at right angles, and offenders are fined. The color of the sidewalk indicates parking restrictions:
red (forbidden), yellow or black (commercial delivery only), white (5 mins only), green (10-30 mins) and blue (disabled drivers only).
Impoundment
Tow away
→ Tel. 621 8605
Rental
Agencies concentrated at airport or around Union Square. From $36/day.
A-One Rent A Car
→ 434 O'Farell St / Taylor St
Tel. 771 3977

FERRIES

Golden Gate Ferries
→ Ferry Bldg (Market St / Embarcadero)
Tel. 923 2000
www.goldengatebridge.org
For a cheap crossing of the bay.
Toward Sausalito
→ Daily except bank hols. Trip 30 mins. Price $5.60.
Toward Larkspur
→ Daily. Trip 45 mins. Price $3.25 ($5.60 at week ends).

AIRPORTS

Information
San Francisco
International Airport
(SFO)
→ Tel. 650 821 8211
On Highway 101,
14 miles south of San
Francisco.
Oakland Airport (OA)
→ Tel. 510 563 3300
17 miles to the south-
east of San Francisco.
Airlines
Daily flights from
London:
British Airways
→ Tel. 0845 773 3377
www.britishairways.com
Virgin Atlantic
→ Tel. 01293 747 747
www.virgin.com/atlantic

AIRPORTS

---

*Except where otherwise
indicated, the prices given
are for a double room with
bathroom and continental
breakfast. Hotel tax (14% of
the price of the room) is not
included. Advance booking
is recommended in the high
season (May-Oct). Most
hotels are concentrated
around Union Square and
Nob Hill.*

RESERVATIONS

Several hotel booking
centers offer special rates,
either by telephone or
Internet. Rates are
negotiable, especially in
the low season (Nov-April).
Hotel Reservation Network
→ Tel. 800 964 6835
www.hoteldiscount.com

YOUTH HOSTEL

**Fort Mason Youth
Hostel** (A D2)
→ Upper Fort Mason Bldg
240. Tel. 771 7277 or
800 909 4776 (toll free)
www.norcalhostels.org
For a bucolic stay in the
heart of Fort Mason: rooms
with 4 to 24 beds,
communal fireplaces, pool
table, and live music in the
evenings at Café Franco.
$23 per person.

Under $90

Grant Hotel (B A6)
→ 753 Bush St /Mason St
Tel. 421 7540
The best value in Nob Hill.
Huge rooms with high
ceilings, thoughtfully and
discreetly decorated:
cream walls, TV, big
bathrooms. No smoking.
From $75.
Astoria (B B6)
→ 510 Bush St / Grant Ave
Tel. 434 8889
Seventy-two simple, clean
rooms in a beautiful
redbrick building close to
Chinatown Gate. $76

($390 for the week).
Halcyon Hotel (D D2)
→ 649 Jones St / Post St
Tel. 929 8033
A hotel with the
atmosphere of a family
boarding house and 25
well-equipped studio-
rooms: TV, small kitchen.
$80–130 (7th night free).
Sheehan Hotel (B A6)
→ 620 Sutter St / Mason St
Tel. 775 6500
The city's biggest indoor
swimming pool is to be
found in this former youth
hostel, now converted into
a hotel. The 65 rooms are
simple but comfortable,
with TV and telephone.
Fitness center. $85–99.
Gaylord (B A6)
→ 620 Jones St / Post St
Tel. 673 8445
A hotel-residence with
a garden and Hispanic
touches (elaborate stucco
porch, sculpted wooden
ceiling in the lobby), where
students from all over the

world come to stay.
Studios with amenities
(kitchenette, bathrooms
and TV). Stays of one week
minimum ($600 a week,
$1200 a month for
2 people).
Stratford Hotel (C B2)
→ 242 Powell St / Geary St
Tel. 397 7080
Classical music and
soothing colors in the
lobby, with 100 or so sober,
modern rooms. From $89.
Savoy Hotel (D D3)
→ 580 Geary St/ Jones St
Tel. 441 2700
On Theatre Row, near
Union Square, this
charming hotel of 83 rooms
has been compared to a
French country inn with
such details as ceiling fans
and feather beds. The
Millennium Restaurant
offers a playful menu of
such healthy and exotic
dishes as Mango Coconut
Curry or Plum Barbecued
Tempeh. $89–$169.

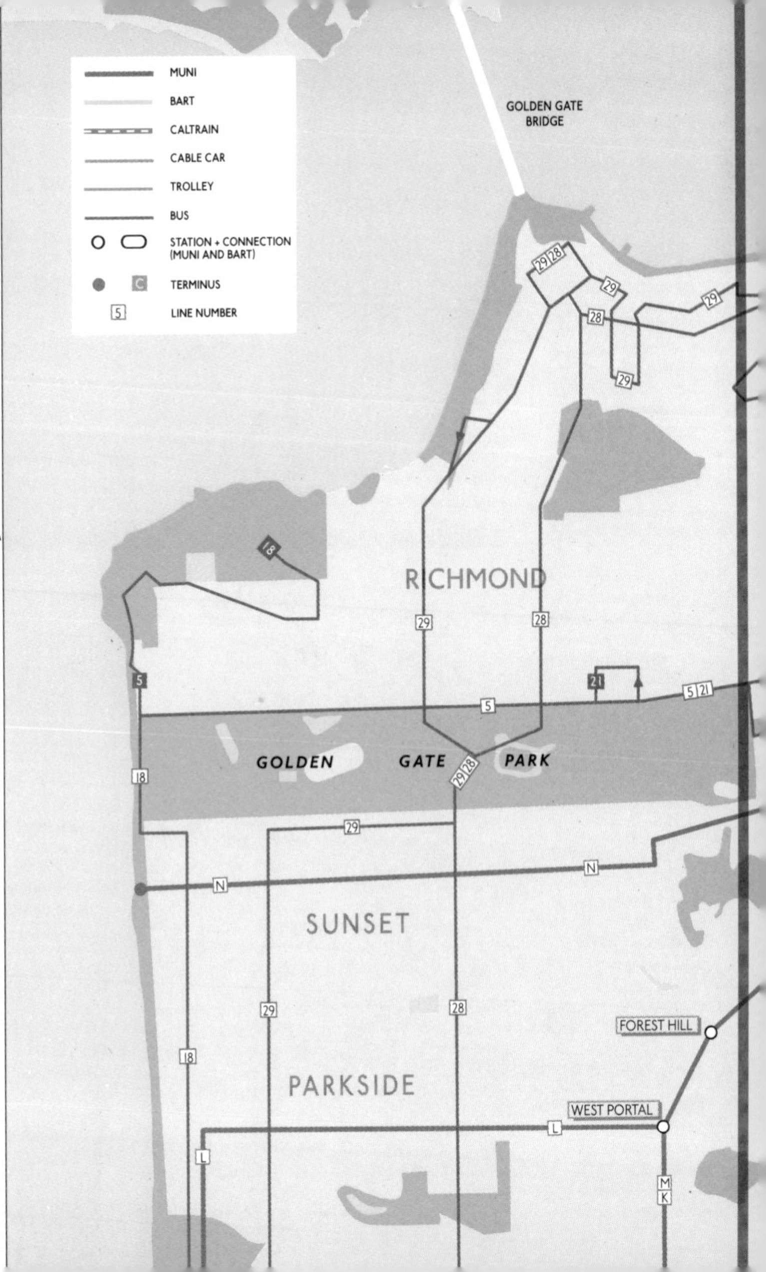

	MUNI
	BART
	CALTRAIN
	CABLE CAR
	TROLLEY
	BUS
○ ⬭	STATION + CONNECTION (MUNI AND BART)
● C	TERMINUS
5	LINE NUMBER

GOLDEN GATE BRIDGE

RICHMOND

GOLDEN GATE PARK

SUNSET

PARKSIDE

FOREST HILL

WEST PORTAL

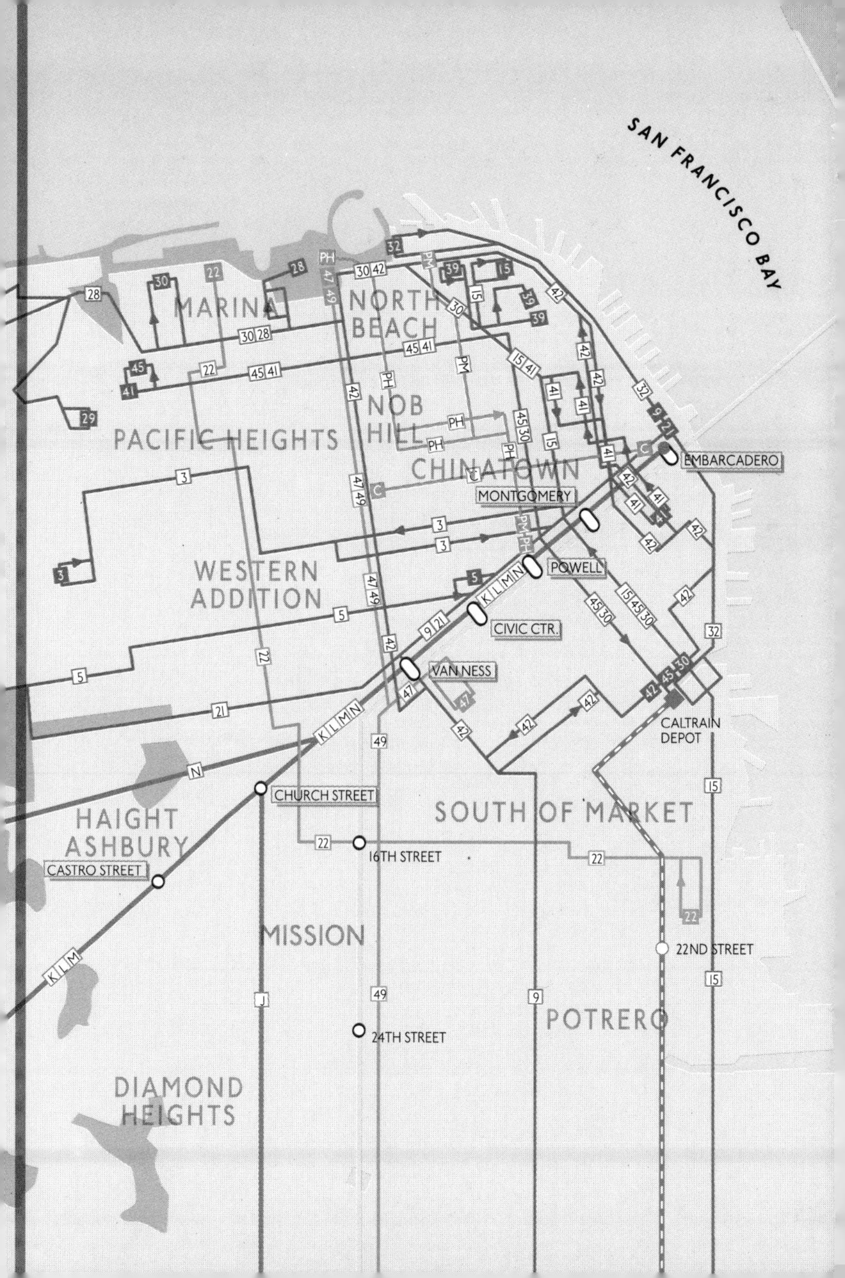

SAN FRANCISCO BAY

MARINA

NORTH BEACH

NOB HILL

PACIFIC HEIGHTS

CHINATOWN

EMBARCADERO

MONTGOMERY

POWELL

WESTERN ADDITION

CIVIC CTR.

VAN NESS

CALTRAIN DEPOT

HAIGHT ASHBURY

CHURCH STREET

SOUTH OF MARKET

CASTRO STREET

16TH STREET

MISSION

24TH STREET

POTRERO

22ND STREET

DIAMOND HEIGHTS

INSIDE A BUS

LUXURY HOTELS

Fairmont Hotel (B A5)
→ *950 Mason St (between Sacramento and California sts). Tel. 772 5000*
www.fairmont.com
The imposing neoclassical façade, across the road from Grace Cathedral, belongs to the most famous and superbly restored hotel in Nob Hill. Splendid lobby with grand staircase and vaulted ceiling. First-class service. Magnificent views over the bay and the Financial District from the tower rooms. Spa, two restaurants; $259 (without view), $319 (with); suites from $499.

The Sherman House (A C4)
→ *2160 Green St, between Filmore and Webster sts Tel. 563 3600*
Located in the residential area of Pacific Heights, this

beautiful Victorian mansion with Bay views and an English garden has 14 rooms and 6 suites decorated with French Second Empire, Jacobean and Biedermeier antiques; canopied beds and fireplaces. No children under 12. $340–$800.

Ritz-Carlton (B B5)
600 Stockton St/Pine St Tel. 296 7465
Located in a neoclassical former insurance building, this grand and luxurious hotel has 336 rooms and suites, with every amenity. It also has a huge fitness center and two restaurants: The Dining Room with French food, the Terrace and also the Lobby Lounge for tea, sushi and cocktails. From $475 up.

Huntington Hotel (B A5)
→ *1075 California St / Taylor St. Tel. 474 5400*
www.huntingtonhotel.com

Luxury and tranquility abound in this rather small but marvelous Art Deco palace (1924). Situated at the top of Nob Hill near the Fairmont. Restaurant, The Big 4, and spa; $310–600.

Mandarin Oriental (B C5)
→ *222 Sansome St / Pine St Tel. 276 9888*
www.mandarin-oriental.com /sanfrancisco
You will get the most magnificent views of the city from this hotel which occupies the 38th to 48th stories of San Francisco's third-highest building. Luxurious. From $500.

Clift (C A2)
→ *495 Geary St / Taylor St Tel. 775 4700*
email:
clift@ianshragerhotels.com
High style chic trendiness from Philippe Starck and Ian Schrager; 374 oversized rooms, the Asia de Cuba restaurant and the famous Redwood bar. From $325.

PUBLIC TRANSPORT

MUNI Network
→ *Tel. 673 6864*
www.sfmuni.com
San Francisco Municipal Railway Network serves every neighborhood with its buses, trains, subway and cable cars. Map ($3) on sale in kiosks and the MUNI agency (949 Presidio Ave).
Timetable
→ *Daily 5.30am–12.30am*
Every 4 to 20 mins, depending on the line.
Single tickets
→ *Price $1.25 (bus and train), $3 (cable car)*
Sold onboard.
MUNI Passport
→ *Price $9 (1 day), $15 (3 days), $20 (7 days)*
A pass giving unlimited access to the entire network (except cable car 50% off only with 7-day pass). Sold at Visitors Bureau (Market St / Powell St) or the MUNI agency.
Bay Area Rapid Transport (BART)
→ *Tel. 992 2278*
A 5-line train network crossing and linking San Francisco with the East Bay (Oakland, Richmond, Fremont, Concord, Berkeley, etc.). Fast and very practical in the city center.
City-center stations
→ *24th St / Mission St; 16th St / Mission St; Civic Center; Montgomery St; Powell St; Embarcadero.*
Tickets
→ *$1.15–4.70*
www.transitinfo.org
Prices depend on the distance. On sale in automatic vending machines in the stations.

TRAIN

TAXIS

The illuminated 'taxi' sign indicates a cab that is free. The 'Taxis only' signs mark taxi stands.

Charges

All the companies charge the same fares.

→ *$2.85, then $1.80/mile (plus $0.45/minute if traffic jam; $0.90/mile for 15-mile journey + outside San Francisco).*

Tipping

Add 10–15% to the cost of the journey.

Radio-taxis

Yellow Cab
→ *Tel. 626 2345*
Veteran's Cab
→ *Tel. 552-1994*

MUNI STATION

YELLOW CAB

Tel. 392 5526
Ever dreamed of owning a yacht? Pretend you do for a couple of nights. Next to Fisherman's Wharf, sleep on a sailboat or motoryacht and be lulled by the rolling of the waters. From $160–400.

Hotel Metropolis (C B3)
→ *25 Mason St / Eddy St Tel. 775 4600*
Elegance, design and comfort in this hotel between Market Street and Union Square. Harmonizing décor (a dominant color on every floor) and care for detail in the rooms (matching carpets and drapes, tiled bathrooms, stylish furniture). Superb views of Portero Hill and the hills of Oakland from the 10th floor. $150.

Hotel Triton (B B6)
→ *342 Grant Ave (between Bush and Sutter sts) Tel. 394 0500*
Luxury, design and originality on the fringes of

Chinatown. Colorful kitsch décor in the lobby (mythological wall paintings, golden pillars) and 'ecological' rooms: air ionizer, biological soaps, towels in natural fabrics. From $239.

Bohème (B B4)
→ *444 Columbus Ave / Green St. Tel. 433 9111*
Go back in time to the days of the Beat Generation. Elegant green and white façade opposite the Greco café, cozy and inviting 1960s décor and tributes to the writer Jack Kerouac. Rooms with old-fashioned furniture, telephone, cable TV, modem outlet. $164.

Archbishop's Mansion (E E1)
→ *1000 Fulton St / Steiner St Tel. 563 7872*
A wonderful pale blue Victorian-style house (1904) opposite Alamo Square Park with 15 delightful rooms (antique French furniture,

drapes, chimney) with lavish fittings (private bathrooms, bathrobe, TV, CD player) and an opera title on each door. $169 including breakfast.

More than $180

White Swan Inn (B A6)
→ *845 Bush St (between Taylor and Mason sts) Tel. 775 1755*
Bow windows and service stairs on the façade, Liberty wallpaper in the lobby, flowers and chimneys in the 26 rooms and suites. England with Union Square on the doorstep. $180 (suite from $275) including afternoon tea.

Hotel Griffon (C E1)
→ *155 Steuart St / Mission St. Tel. 495 2100*
An imaginative conversion of a warehouse (1906) into a charming hotel. Mixture of bricks and wood, Art Deco lamps, mini-bars, bathrobes and CD players in each of

the 57 rooms and 5 suites (3 with terrace). $190–200; suites from $395.

Pan Pacific Hotel (B A6)
→ *500 Post St / Taylor St Tel. 771 8600*
Luxury and modernity a couple of blocks from Union Square. Spectacular atrium from which dizzying stained-glass elevators shop up. TV sets in the marble bathrooms. $265–385.

Campton Place Hotel (B B6)
→ *340 Stockton St, between Post and Sutter sts Tel. 781 5555*
A half block from Union Square, this small (110 rooms and suites) and elegant hotel is the height of luxury right down to the scented candles. The Campton Place Restaurant is celebrated for its innovative Californian cuisine, excellent wine list and quiet ambiance. $335–$470.

The letters (**A, B, C...**) refer to the matching neighborhood section. Letters on their own refer to the spread with useful addresses (restaurants, bars, shops). Letters followed by a star (**A ★**) refer to the spread with a fold-out map and places to visit. The number (**1**) refers to the opening spread **Welcome to San Francisco**.